A Way of Life

A Way of Life

THE STORY OF THE SAMWORTH FAMILY BUSINESS

ADAM LAWRENCE

Published by Samworth Brothers Limited,

Chetwode House, 1 Samworth Way, Leicester Road,

Melton Mowbray, Leicestershire LE13 1GA

Photography: images throughout this publication have been

taken by Paul Brown (www.paulbrownimaging.co.uk) or

retrieved from the Samworth Brothers image archive.

Additional images on pages 32, 40, 42, 43, 48-9 and 51 are reproduced

courtesy of Picture the Past (www.picturethepast.org.uk).

ISBN 978-0-9932838-0-2

Layout and typesetting by Tudor Rose (www.tudor-rose.co.uk).

Printed and bound in Great Britain by Gomer Press Ltd.

www.samworthbrothers.co.uk

This book is dedicated to Frank Samworth (1905-1996), father of the Samworth brothers, first Life President of both Pork Farms and Samworth Brothers, and to his sons Frank (1932-2005) and John (1932-2014), who each played a vital role in establishing our unwavering commitment to quality and manufacturing excellence.

Acknowledgements

With thanks to all Samworth Brothers staff, past and present who helped to compile the two original editions of this book and this updated edition.

Special thanks to Paul Brown for his photography and additional help in compiling this book. A special mention also to Scot Weller and Jo Hartop for their assistance with photography in Cornwall.

Contents

Samworth Brothers: chronology

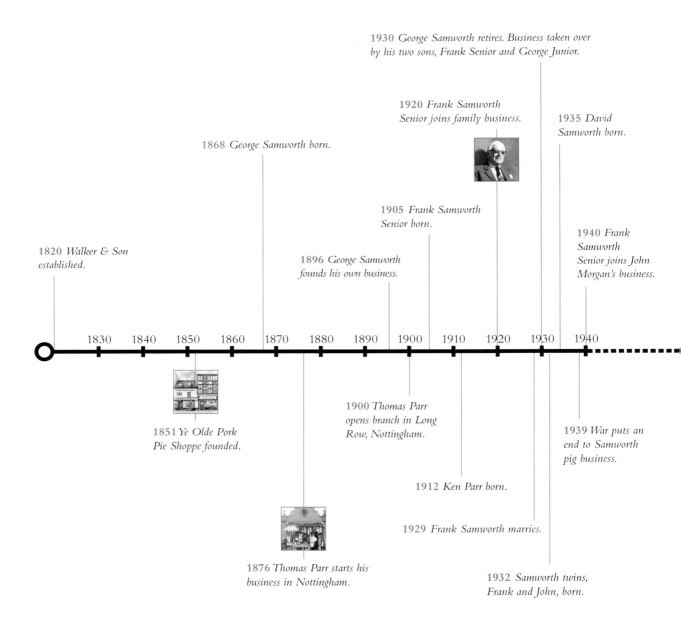

1930 *George Samworth retires. Business taken over by his two sons, Frank Senior and George Junior.*

1920 *Frank Samworth Senior joins family business.*

1935 *David Samworth born.*

1868 *George Samworth born.*

1905 *Frank Samworth Senior born.*

1820 *Walker & Son established.*

1896 *George Samworth founds his own business.*

1940 *Frank Samworth Senior joins John Morgan's business.*

1830 1840 1850 1860 1870 1880 1890 1900 1910 1920 1930 1940

1851 *Ye Olde Pork Pie Shoppe founded.*

1900 *Thomas Parr opens branch in Long Row, Nottingham.*

1939 *War puts an end to Samworth pig business.*

1912 *Ken Parr born.*

1929 *Frank Samworth marries.*

1876 *Thomas Parr starts his business in Nottingham.*

1932 *Samworth twins, Frank and John, born.*

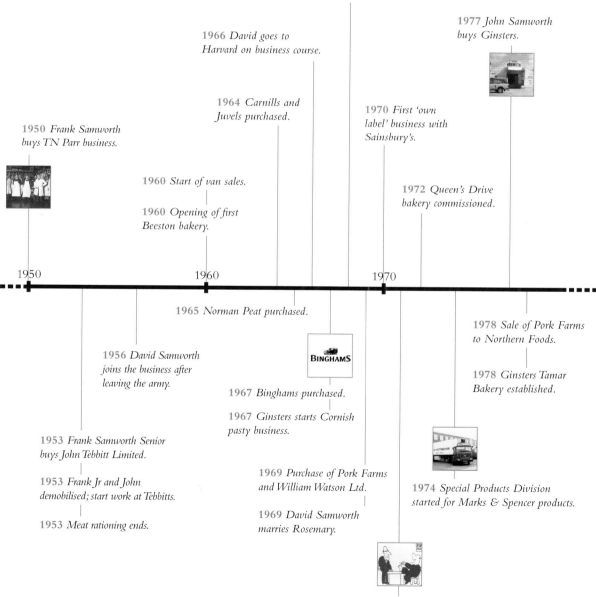

1968 *Frank Samworth retires as Chairman; David becomes Chairman and MD.*

1977 *John Samworth buys Ginsters.*

1966 *David goes to Harvard on business course.*

1964 *Carnills and Juvels purchased.*

1970 *First 'own label' business with Sainsbury's.*

1950 *Frank Samworth buys TN Parr business.*

1960 *Start of van sales.*

1960 *Opening of first Beeston bakery.*

1972 *Queen's Drive bakery commissioned.*

1950

1960

1970

1965 *Norman Peat purchased.*

1956 *David Samworth joins the business after leaving the army.*

BINGHAMS

1978 *Sale of Pork Farms to Northern Foods.*

1978 *Ginsters Tamar Bakery established.*

1967 *Binghams purchased.*

1967 *Ginsters starts Cornish pasty business.*

1953 *Frank Samworth Senior buys John Tebbitt Limited.*

1953 *Frank Jr and John demobilised; start work at Tebbitts.*

1953 *Meat rationing ends.*

1969 *Purchase of Pork Farms and William Watson Ltd.*

1969 *David Samworth marries Rosemary.*

1974 *Special Products Division started for Marks & Spencer products.*

1971 *Flotation of Pork Farms.*

1997 Brian Stein appointed Group Managing Director.

1997 Samworth Brothers Distribution opens Woodside Distribution Depot.

1997 Kensey Foods created.

1997 Chetwode House built.

1997 David Samworth appointed High Sheriff of Leicestershire.

1980 David Samworth becomes chair of Meat & Livestock Commission.

1984 David takes chairmanship of Ginsters. He also becomes Deputy Lieutenant of Leicestershire.

1995 Brian Stein joins Group.

1999 John Samworth retires from Samworth Brothers.

1993 Bradgate sandwich bakery opens at Beaumont Leys.

1999 Brian Stein appointed CEO.

1986 Walker & Son acquired.

1999 Tamar Foods is demerged from Ginsters.

1989 Commissioning of Charnwood Bakery at Beaumont Leys.

1999 Kettleby Foods bakery opens for business.

1980

1990

1998 Melton Foods opens on new Melton Mowbray site.

1987 Ginsters Lynher Bakery opens at Callington.

1985 Company name changed to Samworth Brothers.

1996 Death of Frank Samworth Senior.

1992 Ginsters' third bakery (Kensey) opens at Launceston.

1996 Mark Samworth appointed MD of Midshire Foods.

1985 David Samworth appointed CBE.

1992 Westward Laboratories established at Callington.

1996 Holdings Board established.

1992 Ye Olde Pork Pie Shoppe re-opened by Samworth Brothers.

1996 Bradgate voted Best Factory by Management Today.

1981 David resigns from Northern Foods and Pork Farms.

1994 Mark Samworth joins Group.

2000 *Group turnover
exceeds £300 million.*

2013 *Samworth Brothers Sports
Opportunity Fund is launched.*

2004 *Completion of £20 million
redevelopment of Lynher Bakery.*

2013 *Samworth Brothers Charity Challenge
fundraising total reaches £1 million.*

2008 *Cold Call established.*

2008 *Blueberry Foods established.*

2011 *Samworth Brothers
wins the Family Business
of the Year Award at the
Private Business Awards.*

2015 *Samworth Brothers
Distribution becomes Samworth
Brothers Supply Chain.*

2000

2010

2014 *Soreen is acquired by the Group.*

2014 *Death of John Samworth.*

2009 *David Samworth receives a
knighthood for services to charity.*

2014 *Bradgate Bakery expands with the
building of Bradgate Bakery Ashton Green.*

2014 *Walkers Midshire Foods becomes two
businesses: Walkers Deli and Walkers Sausage Co.*

2005 *David Samworth retires
from Chairmanship, to be
replaced by Nick Linney.*

2003 *Group turnover above £400 million.*

2003 *Saladworks opens in Leicester.*

2012 *Brooksby Foods established.*

2003 *Samworth Brothers wins
Leicestershire's Business of the Decade.*

2012 *Brian Stein retires and Lindsey Pownall
takes over as Group Chief Executive.*

Foreword

by Lindsey Pownall
Group Chief Executive, Samworth Brothers

This is a very special book.

It has been compiled to coincide with the celebration of the 80th birthday of Sir David Samworth, President of Samworth Brothers Limited. In the two previous editions of this book each foreword has largely focused on Samworth Brothers Limited; however, on this occasion, I want to write about Sir David Samworth who, with his brother John, is the inspiration behind this wonderful business.

As Sir David celebrates his 80th birthday this year, I too reach a milestone of 20 years in Samworth Brothers. It is through these 20 years that I have come to understand the unique qualities that Sir David has, which have created this incredible business of which I am very proud to be Group Chief Executive.

Over these years I have watched and learned from the way Sir David, an entrepreneur, painstakingly weaved the culture, values and standards that he wanted in the business. Sir David deployed a huge range of distinctive and powerful tactics in this mission, many of which I reflect on with a smile and many others I unashamedly admit to adopting myself. There are three particular tactics I want to mention here. Collectively they illustrate Sir David's unique (and highly successful) approach and the strong values that he has infused so robustly into the business.

Sir David always made everything very personal and people simply never wanted to let him down, not necessarily through fear (although you could experience the odd white knuckle moment), but because of the enormous respect and affection they had for him. In a filing cabinet I have kept all the letters Sir David has written to me over the years. I, like many of my colleagues, keep these letters because they are always hand written, always of a congratulatory nature, always recognising some achievement or other. They are beautifully expressed, warm and sensitive. The lesson I learned from this was, always find time to personalise things as this is very motivational for your people, as indeed all my letters from Sir David are for me.

ABOVE: *Sir David Samworth at a Melton Foods Long Service Awards event, at Leicester racecourse, in 2014.*

Sir David's close attention to detail and his emphasis on ensuring that personal touch were demonstrated whenever he made one of his regular site visits. Sir David had these visits down to a fine art and he used them to educate his teams about values. If a car parking space had been reserved at the door, Sir David would deliberately park in the first available space in the staff car park. He would always test us on the percentage of soft landscaping to ensure the external areas had the correct look and feel. He always insisted on a trip to the staff restaurant, so that he could check the quality of the food being served.

The highlight of the tour for everyone was when he entered the bakery and staff would watch his every move. Sir David always smiled, joked and laughed with everyone and the warmth he exuded was received with great affection. Never rushed, his visits were designed to let as many people as possible see him. This was how he reinforced his family values, by being visible and real. When I was a Managing Director my sites would host many visitors during a year but no visit would ever be quite as memorable as the Sir David Samworth visit.

When it came to standards, Sir David was very clear. Quality was absolutely at the top of his agenda. It wasn't difficult creating the Samworth Brothers logo some 19 years ago. It was simply a business

truth inspired by Sir David: 'Quality is a way of life'. Not only was quality instilled into the Samworth Brothers team, but Sir David was never afraid to remind the retailers, our customers, of their responsibility to create quality food for consumers under their own brands. Sir David has championed, on behalf of the industry, a quality ethos firmly rooted in producing excellent food where taste is of paramount importance, as is producing it in excellent facilities.

The challenge of the foreword written by The Rt. Hon. the Lord Walker of Worcester MBE PC in 1996 was whether the business would be able to adapt over time (see Appendix 3 on page 185). I can honestly say that the principles on which Sir David and John Samworth built their business have and will always serve the business well. To instil a culture where being personal, sensitive and caring, all the hallmarks of a lovely family, was not only brilliant, but authentic as well. The Samworth family are all these things and the wider family's involvement in the business is always a pleasure to host.

Recent times have been hugely challenging for the business as the UK food retailers face stormy waters. As we sail, navigating a course to find clear blue water for both our business and for our customers, it is Sir David's values and quality ethos that will always guide us to success.

Introduction

by Mark Samworth
Group Director, Samworth Brothers

Our family is privileged to own a business that can do so much good for so many people. Having a family firm gives us the chance to be involved in a great commercial and social enterprise — and it's in our DNA. Whether individual family members contribute as colleagues of the business or only as supportive owners, we are all committed to owning and investing in Samworth Brothers in the very long term.

We have been very fortunate in our family to have had passionate and talented people to drive the group forward. In particular, David and John's extraordinary abilities and close working relationship re-grew the business with the purchase of Ginsters in 1977 (and later Walkers in 1986) after deciding to sell Pork Farms to Northern Foods. A turnover of £1 million then has become £1 billion today.

Mine is the fourth generation to have been involved in the business. All three of my sisters have worked in it but I am now the only family member to be actively involved in the management of the group. Given that every member of the fifth generation is aged ten or under, this is unlikely to change before the next instalment of this book! So, of course, we have welcomed people from outside the family to run Samworth Brothers. Brian Stein was the first to do so and Lindsey Pownall now leads the business. Their appointments, though, have not come about because of an interregnum between generations of Samworths — we could never attract good people if that was all we could offer. Rather, the family believes that the business must have the very best people in the industry to work in it and lead it; above all, we want the business to succeed, and success depends on having the right people.

One of the great strengths of being a family business is that the family can develop the values and culture of the business and recruit good people who share those same values. In Samworth Brothers the culture is usually expressed as us all having a deep regard for people, a passion for quality and service, and an awareness that investment, growth and opportunity can only happen in businesses that are profitable. At its heart, it is a simple business philosophy and it reflects our ambition to grow good businesses in the right ways.

This ambition is rooted in our twin beliefs that healthy businesses grow and that owning a healthy business is the biggest social impact that our family can have. A healthy business creates improved prospects for its people, new orders for its suppliers, new revenue streams for its customers and new products and services for consumers. Healthy businesses are an important part of their communities; they pay taxes to support the wider social structure and they donate time, money and energy to local causes. Successive generations of the family have found ways to grow the business — often in very difficult times, as you will read — and our instinct is always to pursue profitable growth through doing the right things for the consumer, our customers and our people.

The desire for growth has meant we have pursued different commercial strategies at different times — the strategies employed in local markets by George Samworth in the early 1900s were necessarily different from those adopted by Frank Snr. in regional markets after the war, and again by John, Frank Jr. and David as they grew in national markets in the 1970s onwards. It is easy to think that such rapid and regular changes of course might indicate a business with no sense of long term direction. But the opposite is true; any firm that aspires to prosperity in the long term has to accept change as a way of life and must regularly hone its responses to the market. What remains a constant, however, is our commitment to our values, our culture and our attitude to doing business — they are the things that make us unique.

Why make this point? Because to do the right thing for the consumer and for our customers in today's market means that we are adapting the way we work to reflect their priorities. Samworth Brothers is bigger and more complex than it has ever been before, and so we have to look harder to see how to do the right things to drive healthy growth. Happily, though, the consumer and our customers are signposting the way: the complexity that drove range proliferation, consumer confusion and supply chain inefficiency is being replaced by a clarity of offer that must reduce costs and improve consumer engagement. We are therefore working hard to do better the things that the consumer most values and to stop doing those things that they don't — it is the very essence of continuous improvement.

We are proud of the way we operate — in our many businesses we have motivated people who are close to their customers who, in turn, trust them to do an excellent job. But we must also address the weaknesses that are inherent in a decentralised group. Individual businesses run locally are powerful vehicles which deliver great customer service but they are not always of a scale to get best value in purchasing or to be able to afford the full costs of real consumer insight, to give just two examples. However when we talk about bringing our scale to bear for the benefit of our customers, 'the Samworth Way' is not to centralise the business. It is to collaborate, person to person, and to pool resources so that we have a common Samworth Brothers approach wherever it makes sense to do so. It is both to use much better the new technology that is available whilst also spending more time in face to face discussions with each other.

This is happening across the group and will enhance the authority of people at each business because the benefits of scale can and should be shared across our group rather than hoarded at the centre.

Everyone in our industry is adapting to a very tough marketplace which is not going to get any easier. Yet the values which are becoming increasingly important to the consumer and our customers — clarity, quality, collaboration, flexibility, honesty — are all values that we recognise as core to the way we think. They reflect what should be the natural strengths of a family business which invests for the long term, which is stable and financially independent, and whose ambition is to provide healthy growth for our people and customers across the generations.

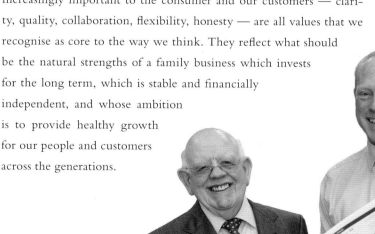

THIS PAGE: *George Samworth Senior, founder, in about 1933.*

RIGHT: *The Samworth family on Frank Senior's wedding day, March 1929. Left to right (standing) Mabel, Doris, Evelyn, George Junior, Hilda and Frank; (seated) George Senior and his wife, Catherine.*

FAR RIGHT: *Phyllis Samworth (née Perkins) 1906-1996. Wife of Frank Samworth Senior.*

THE ORIGINS

In the 1890s, the young George Samworth must have been a familiar figure to many of the pig farmers of the West Midlands. Arriving by bicycle or train, he would buy up their livestock to sell on to the pork butchers of Birmingham. George and his bicycle were the beginnings of a business still thriving over 120 years later.

Born in Birmingham in 1868, George Samworth left school at the age of 11, and began working with a consortium of Birmingham pig dealers; men who were engaged in buying pigs from farmers and reselling them, still alive, to pork butchers' shops in the Birmingham area. His working week amounted to some 65 hours and his wage about ten shillings (50p) a week. George did well in this job and gained a thorough knowledge in the trade of pig dealing. In 1890 he married Catherine and in 1896 he started in business on his own. Travelling around by train and bicycle, he would visit farms, cutting deals with the farmers before arranging to sell the pigs — still alive, remember — to pork butchers in Birmingham, of whom there were over 100 in the city alone.

His marriage produced two sons, George and Frank, and four daughters, Evelyn, Mabel, Doris and Hilda. Frank Samworth joined his father's growing business at the age of 14, as his elder brother George

Pictures from the Walkers archive illustrating what the meat business looked like in the 1920s when George and his sons were developing their family business.

BELOW: *A display of winning carcasses from a fat stock show at Walkers shop, Christmas 1920.*

RIGHT: *A Walkers slaughterhouse c. 1925.*

had done before him. When Frank joined his father, World War I meat rationing had just ended and meat was decontrolled. As a result, retail butchers were enjoying a seller's market in satisfying the hunger for meat. Together the Samworths, father and sons, travelled all over the United Kingdom buying pigs on their own behalf and, later, as agents for others. Their purchases were loaded up by the vending farmer and sent by rail to Birmingham, where their time of arrival was announced to the Samworths by telegram: 'So many pigs despatched today.' When the animals reached Birmingham station they were collected by the Samworths and driven 'on the hoof' through the streets of the city for delivery to individual customers. These were small pork butchers who, until relatively recently, bought live pigs which they themselves slaughtered in small abattoirs behind their shops.

Frank Samworth could remember the excitement of urging and prodding herds of agitated pigs through the crowded city — dodging and holding up trams, carts and wheelbarrows. Behind him rode his brother George in the 'pig float', a small cart for transporting any lame pigs and giving a lift to any that might falter. It was during this period

of direct dealing in the pork butchers trade that Frank Samworth gained much of his knowledge of pork meat and pork products, for most pork butchers at that time produced their own pork pies, sausages, black puddings and the like. Throughout the inter-war years the business flourished and Frank related that it was during this period that he learned from his father all that formed the basis of the firm's economics and ethics and the business philosophy that guided him thereafter. He also became aware of the values, assets and advantages of a family run business. George Samworth retired in 1930 and the business was taken over by his two sons.

In 1929 Frank married Phyllis Perkins and set up home in Moseley village in Birmingham, then 'a lovely, quiet little place'. Here were born twin brothers Frank and John Samworth in 1932, David in 1935 and their sister Barbara in 1937.

Following the outbreak of war in 1939 the normal peacetime system of distribution of meat from producers to retailers via the wholesalers was brought under direct government control. Wholesale meat markets were closed and the control of all foods was vested in the newly-created Ministry of Food. This brought an abrupt end to the business of George

Samworth & Sons, and saw the sons go their own separate ways. The future of Frank Samworth in the meat business we shall follow in some detail: his brother, George Junior, also continued in the industry after the war, buying a bacon curing business in the Black Country town of Tipton. Sadly he died at the early age of 58, in 1958.

Frank Samworth went to work as a General Manager for a close friend, John Morgan, a pork butcher who owned a leading Birmingham firm manufacturing bacon, sausages and other pork products. It was through his employment with Morgans that Frank Samworth became interested in the manufacture and retailing of pork products — especially pork pies. He also mastered the craft of bacon curing and formulated his own recipes for curing brine.

In 1945, Morgan, wanting to retire, offered Frank a partnership with himself as sleeping partner — an arrangement that precluded the future possibility of turning Morgans into a Samworth family business. Frank had some experience of being a part of a family business, an

BELOW: *The Samworth brothers at play, Edgbaston, Easter 1946. Left to right, John, David, Frank. At the wicket is Warwickshire's 'Tiger' Smith, a former England wicket keeper.*

PRIVATE CASH BOOK.
T. N. PARR. LTD.

1950						1950					
Nov 22	To	F.o.P. Somworth – Shares purchased	P.L / 15,000			Oct 30	By	Preliminary Expenses	N.L.		
4		Cashings (Takings)	Ex 4/ 2,278 2 4			Nov 6		Midland Market Purch	25/ 1 16		
11		Takings	1. 3,976 11 6					Wages	270 8 11		
18		Takings	1. 2,888 12					Sundry	48/ 3 3		
25			4903 5 5			11		Wages	274 16 3		
30			759 16 1					Purchases Mid Market	25/ 3 11		
Dec 9			11 3,093 12 8					Sundry	28/ 19 6		
16			11 1,750 18 4			18		Wages	294 14 11		
23			11 3767 18 5			25		Purchases Mid Market	25/ 3 11 2		
30			4 1272 3					Wages	298 8 9		
6		Bad Debts	11 7 11 7			30		Wages	66/ 12 7		
7			11 9 15 9					Cleaning and Towel	48/ 2 2		
9			11 28 5 7					Sundries	48/ 1 5 6		
11			11 243 1			Dec 9		Wages	N/ 25 7 6		
12			11 4 5			Nov 9		Stamp Duty	30/ 100		
13			11 35 19 2			30		Deposit to Vendor	31/ 5750		
15			11 6 6 8			22		Balance of Purch Money	1,713 13 2		
18			11 19			23		Crushed & Tomkinson – Re Share Capital	30/ 794		
21			11 15 12			25		Interest on Balance of Purch Money			
23			11 80 7 8					and Rent for Brotherhood Room	31/ 99 11 6		
23			11 14 7 2			Dec 5		Cheque book	7/ 2		
27			11 615 8			Dec 31		Bank Charges	7/ 220 11		
28			11 40 1 6			Dec 22		Xmas Boxes	48/ 100		
30			11 2 10 4			27		Cheque book	7/ 2		
Dec		Bacon Sales	Ex 12 8901 4 2			1951 Jan 1		Cheque book	7/ 5		
Dec		Bird Sales	21 1581 7 11								
1951 Jan 6		Takings	22 1941 9 3								
13		Takings	22 1963 4 9								
			54759 19 11						59972 1		

experience that had implanted in him a reluctance to work for others. Further, it was only by way of developing a family business that Frank could envisage the building of something big. He therefore refused Morgan's offer and began to look around for a business he could buy.

For four years or so Frank continued in his position as manager with Morgans while seeing that his three sons were well grounded in the basics of the trade he had chosen. The family's friends included some who were also in the meat and bakery trade and they too gave the boys occasional employment. John Samworth spent some of his spare time helping out in the bakery of one such friend. Here he was instructed by the owner: 'I don't care how you make the things — you can make 'em good or make 'em bad, but be sure to make 'em the same every day'. All three boys went to Hallfield School in Birmingham and then to Uppingham School in Rutland where they all did well.

During his years with John Morgan, Frank Samworth had done more than dream of starting out on his own, for as the Morgans business thrived, so did he until, by 1949, he had amassed enough money to buy a meat business outright — although his timing was not ideal. The war had ended in 1945 but meat rationing continued until 1953. Meat products companies were earning a lot of money and were very rarely up for sale. A salesman visiting Morgans in the summer of 1950 mentioned to Frank that a meat products firm with which he dealt was in difficulties and up for sale. It was, he said, an old-established, highly reputable family business which, because of meat rationing, had declined during the war. The name of the firm was TN Parr Ltd of Nottingham.

Frank inspected TN Parr, made a quick decision in its favour and agreed a price of £30,000 with proprietor Percy Parr. He approached the Midland Bank and got the backing he needed and, in September 1950, bought the business outright. In doing so, he joined the 80 pork butchers operating in Nottingham at the time. Thus the beginnings of the Samworth family business came about, through the willingness to pursue opportunities, even in the face of significant risks, because both George and his son Frank believed that it was better to work for the family in a business that it owned than to work for other people or for Government.

LEFT (TOP): *TN Parr's Mansfield Road bakery in 1950. Second from left, David Samworth; third from left, Frank Samworth Junior; fourth from right, Percy Parr; second from right; Frank Samworth Senior.*

LEFT: *Frank Samworth's cash book, 1950.*

T. N. PARR

Pork Butcher,
Ham & Bacon
Curer,
Sausage & Pork Pie
MANUFACTURER,

155, MANSFIELD ROAD
AND 2, ANGEL ROW,

NOTTINGHAM.

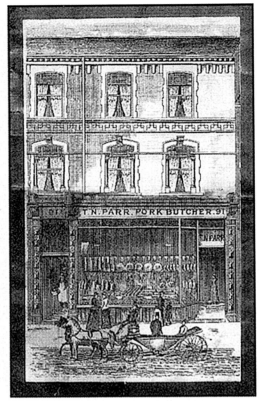

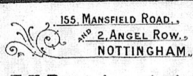

155, MANSFIELD ROAD,
AND 2, ANGEL ROW,
NOTTINGHAM.

T. N. PARR begs to thank his numerous patrons for their past favours, and to state that every care is taken to maintain the reputation enjoyed for many years past for the choicest quality, at moderate prices, only the best meat is sold, and all goods are manufactured on the premises in perfect hygienic conditions and cleanliness under strict personal supervision, and are to be thoroughly depended on

CHOICEST QUALITY

FOR BREAKFAST
LUNCHEON, TEA,

FOR PARTIES
PICNICS &
OUTINGS

NO TABLE
COMPLETE WITHOUT ONE

COOKED HOME CURED HAMS
ALWAYS ON HAND.

SIMPLY DELICIOUS.

ONLY BEST
HOME FED
MEAT USED

NONE BETTER,

SELDOM
EQUALLED,

NEVER EXCELLED.

A FAMILY BUSINESS

Frank Senior and his sons Frank Junior, John and David Samworth each played a valuable and distinctive role in the business. In 1950, as Britain started to pull itself out of post war austerity, a new Samworth era began. The TN Parr years were vital in laying the groundwork for future success.

The business that Frank Samworth bought in 1950 had a long and proud history. Thomas Naylor Parr established his first pork butcher's shop at 155 Mansfield Road, Nottingham in the 1870s, where he sold pork and pork products under the sign of 'TN Parr'. Within a short time he had become locally famous for the flavour and quality of his pies — a fame that was soon to spread throughout Nottingham. His regular baking times became known in the district and housewives queued along Mansfield Road to buy his pies as they emerged hot from the oven. Over time the business expanded to three shops, passing to his sons, Tom and Percy, who continued the family business during the war years.

Tom Parr died in 1943 and, when his son Ken returned at the end of World War II in 1945, his Uncle Percy was running the business. This was not to Ken's liking for he and Percy had never got on well together. After a short spell of work at Mansfield Road, Ken Parr decided to make his own way and began looking for something he could afford to buy.

Situated on the outskirts of the town, the two small run-down butchers' shops Ken Parr bought and turned around had, by 1947,

PREVIOUS PAGE (LEFT): TN Parr's four-page circular, about 1885. The upper right hand frame shows the shop and bakery in Mansfield Road, Nottingham.

PREVIOUS PAGE (RIGHT): David Samworth's 21st birthday at George Hotel, Nottingham, 1956. Left to right, Ivy Perkins, David, Phyllis, Frank Senior, Barbara, John, Frank Junior.

BELOW: A Parr's butcher's shop in Radcliffe-on-Trent, Nottingham, in the 1920s.

become amongst the busiest of their kind in Nottingham. Deciding that the time was ripe to move nearer the centre, he came across a small pork butcher's shop in Pelham Street named Pork Farms. Ken 'liked the name' and bought it on the spot for £2,000. Thus was established the firm of Pork Farms which was to play a crucial part in the subsequent history of the Samworth family.

Four years after Ken Parr had left his family's business to go it alone, Frank Samworth purchased TN Parr. The business he had bought was still housed in the Mansfield Road premises and also had three branches in Nottingham. With a total staff of 15, its turnover was £250,000 a year, showing a net profit of £10,000. One of its most valuable assets, and that which attracted Frank Samworth, was its repute for producing the best pork pie in Nottingham — for at that time the neck-and-neck rivalry between Parr's and its offspring Pork Farms for this accolade had not yet developed.

Frank found the business in a poor state. Under the management of Percy Parr, the firm's product quality had been well maintained, but the business side had deteriorated over the years. The purchase of

ABOVE: *The TN Parr Special Products Division at Lilac Grove, Beeston which included a successful van sales and distribution business.*

Parr's marked the foundation of the modern Samworth family business, and the time chosen to establish it was both fortunate and significant. Wartime controls of food were finally being removed; and it was also the beginning of the decade, 1950-60, during which wage rises kept ahead of the Retail Price Index by almost 100 per cent, and when a new generation of working women helped to create the income that was to power the great consumer boom of the 1960s. It was also the time when the foundations were laid for the present success of the British chain stores and supermarkets.

On Frank's first day at TN Parr he had discovered that in the sandstone cellars there stood a 20-side capacity bacon-curing vat, unused for several years. He lost no time in filling the vat with a brine made to his own recipe and producing his first consignment of bacon. Over the following years more vats were installed at Mansfield Road and the increased production sold to bacon wholesalers. By 1955 a total output of 500 sides a week had been attained, and an even larger outlet was sought. Frank Samworth knew of one prospective wholesale customer who supplied some 6,000 sides of bacon a week to the retail trade. This was Allied Suppliers of London, owner of a number of chain-store grocers that included such (then) household names as Maypole, Liptons, International Stores and Home & Colonial Stores.

In London, Frank Samworth was welcomed by Allied Supplies' Buying Director, George Highton, who told him that Allied was looking for new suppliers. Allied had its own transport system and so could collect from Parr's. 'I'll take all you've got, and pick it up from you.'

Like most owners of a business, Frank Samworth had hoped from the start that his children would one day want to enter the business with him, but he never pressured them to do so. And so he continued the regime he had begun at Morgans. At home he kept them informed of day-to-day developments and related to them the exciting and challenging aspects of running a business. It was with the future of his sons in mind that, early in 1953, he decided to expand through the acquisition for £23,600 of John Tebbitt Ltd, an old-established family firm of pig slaughterers and bacon curers operating at Cradley Heath in Staffordshire. The Tebbitt plant had a throughput of some 75 pigs a week and, in addition to bacon curing, manufactured the usual range of pork butchers' products. One important aspect of the purchase of Tebbitts was that the firm ran three sales vans that supplied a number of small butchers and grocers in the surrounding towns and villages. This was Frank Samworth's first experience of van sales and it was to have an important effect on the future of the Samworth business.

One hangover from World War II was conscription (which lasted until 1959). When his turn came in 1951, Frank Samworth Junior joined the ranks of the Royal Artillery, and was later commissioned as a Second Lieutenant. During the same year, John went into the Royal Armoured Corps and was stationed in Germany as a Corporal. In 1954 David joined the Royal Leicestershire Regiment, was sent to Khartoum as a Second Lieutenant and served as aide-de-camp to the Governor-General. John left the army in September 1953 and two days later was boning out shoulders of pork at Tebbitts in Cradley Heath. In time, the family team was completed with the demobilisation of Frank and David — for all three had by then decided to join the business.

LEFT: *David Samworth, far right, accompanying the Governor-General during his period in the Royal Leicestershire Regiment in Khartoum in Sudan.*

ABOVE: *A reminder of TN Parr history in Glasshouse Street, Nottingham.*

The brothers were not working at Tebbitts by chance or for the firm's convenience, for Frank Samworth had seen a hidden advantage in the purchase. Being a self-contained operation, it was an ideal training school for the brothers to learn all aspects of the practical operations involved in pork production and the manufacture of pork products, even down to the running of a small bakery.

By 1958, with total profits running at £30,000, Parr's production capacity had been brought to its limit and it was clear to Frank Samworth that better manufacturing facilities must be created. Tebbitts was sold as all available resources, both financial and family, were needed to build and equip the new facility.

The plan was for a purpose-built plant in Nottingham to handle the whole manufacturing operation: killing pigs, cutting, boning, curing hams and bacon, making sausages and pies. A suitable site was found at Lilac Grove in Beeston in Nottingham and there a 45,000 square foot food-processing unit was built by the Copenhagen firm of NE Wernberg. Its cost was the then considerable sum of £300,000.

These were anxious days for the family, its financial resources stretched to the limit, with a bank overdraft of £100,000. Frank Samworth had always used the same bankers, the Birmingham New Street branch of Midland Bank (which, as HSBC, Samworth Brothers still uses today), and it was unfortunate that at this particular time the branch had a most uncooperative manager. On hearing of Frank's plans he agreed the credit facility but warned: 'If this overdraft goes one penny over £100,000, I shall not honour your cheques!' This resulted in a very tense situation at Mansfield Road and, when the bank statements arrived every Tuesday and Friday, they were opened with great trepidation. But disaster was averted due to the increasing sales and good cashflow. The Beeston plant was completed in 1960 and was acknowledged as being one of the best of its kind in the UK.

Until then the firm's policy had been to acquire or open its own shops to keep pace with increasing production — but a great many more shops would have been required to make the new bakery economically viable. At that time shops were costing some £5,000 to set up while, as had been learned from Tebbitts, a single van calling on outside retail shops could be put on the road for only £500. And so, with the completion of the Beeston plant in 1960, a long-term plan was drawn up to develop a wide-ranging van selling operation.

The operation was taken over by David Samworth who, starting with a single van, soon built up a substantial business with independent butchers, grocers, corner shops and off-licences. By the early 1960s it had become clear to Frank Samworth and his sons that a period of rationalisation for the meat industry was on its way. So it was agreed that the business would benefit from a further programme of expansion by acquisition. The Nottingham firm of Carnill, a small pork butcher's with a van sales operation, and Juvels, a Nottingham bakery, were both acquired in 1964, followed by Norman Peat, a chain of butcher's shops in Sheffield in 1965 and Bingham's Cooked Meats, the Sheffield-based makers of Bingham's Meat Spread in 1967.

The board of TN Parr was composed of Frank Samworth and his three sons. Frank Senior acted as chairman and did all the buying. Frank Junior managed the making-up processes and the bakery, while John supervised and developed the van delivery service and the shops. He was also responsible for the coordination of the subsidiary companies, each of which he inspected and reported on every week. Having the wider business vision and a sound familiarity with finance, David concerned himself with general management, administration and accountancy. Most of the business and decision-making was done informally on a family basis and adopted officially at the regular Thursday afternoon board meetings. Frank Senior was later to claim that, in the 20 years leading up to his retirement, every boardroom decision was unanimous!

But with all the informality, Frank Senior played his part in the everyday business of running a company, exercising what is now known as the 'old style' of management by personally and directly supervising many aspects of the business. He had an eagle eye for detail, insisting, for example, that the directors (that is, his sons) met together every morning to open the post. Another family meeting took place at eight o'clock every morning for the purpose of tasting the firm's

products for flavour, filling texture, pastry thickness and baking quality. This custom is still carried out at all Samworth Brothers production units — except that tasting is now a continual process with many samples of each product being examined and tasted by several of the group staff.

RIGHT: *Frank Samworth Senior, 1905-1996.*

ABOVE: *The Samworths (father and sons) examining pork pie production. Left to right, David, John, Frank Junior and Frank Senior.*

TN Parr had also now grown into a very substantial business. Its Beeston plant supplied its own 19 shops and a fleet of vans covered Nottingham, Birmingham, Sheffield and the areas around. With this expansion a more comprehensive system of management became necessary and David Samworth began looking around for likely trainee managers. In 1964 the first of these to join was Wally Huckle who had been a Unilever management trainee and played cricket and hockey with the Samworth brothers.

Starting first in the bakery, Wally later went on, in 1975, to become Managing Director of TN Parr and in 1977 Managing Director of Pork Farms.

By 1964, Frank Samworth had realised that he needed to step back from the family business, to take life a little easier but also to enable his sons to plough their own furrow. He continued as Chairman but confined his activities to the buying of meat, bacon and other fresh produce. But the brothers realised that the managerial experience they possessed had been gained in the army. Their commercial working background had been confined to the rather spontaneous 'family style' of running a business; none had any experience of working with a big company.

David thus decided to undertake a course in business management at the Harvard Business School in Massachusetts. On his return, it was unanimously agreed by the family that he should act as Managing Director and the result was a family management team that was a model combination of abilities and talents. David possessed management sense and the capability for planning strategy; John was a most suitable complement to this, being a person who understood the hearts of the employees and the characteristics of the customers. Together with the shop supervisor, John was continually on the lookout for, and opening, new shops in neighbouring towns. He was also responsible for fitting out these shops and managing them himself until they became well established and reached the level of sales for which they had been budgeted. Frank Junior was best at home with 'things' — and did exceptionally well as production manager. He it was who kept all the shops and van sales supplied with fresh produce of the highest quality.

David's first move was to introduce a weekly profit and loss system which, until then, was practically unknown in the meat industry — mainly because it took two full days to take stock efficiently; it being then the custom to run stocks down at the end of each financial year, take stock, and build up again. At first, David's idea met with some resistance until it was found to work. Later the same procedure was successfully applied to the shops and was eventually adopted across the industry.

Through all these developments the Samworth commitment to quality was sustained (and remains to this day). With the rigid maintenance of this policy, Samworth products gained a reputation for consistent quality as opposed to undistinguished, run-of-the-mill, price-cutting products. The firm's sales slogan at this time was 'Quality and Freshness' and the freshness was maintained by recommending customers to buy less rather than more. This feel for product quality was summed up by David Samworth in 1971: "I believe there is a danger that quality controllers will weigh a product, measure it, smell it, do everything with it, in fact, except taste it. We believe it is the job of top management to ensure quality of our pies, sausages, hams and bacon and we do it by the best possible method. Every day we eat our products, and those of some of our competitors."

PORK FARMS

As TN Parr developed, one business rival often loomed large,
Pork Farms. The two companies had a shared history that gave a
further intensity to their commercial battles.

COOKED MEATS

Pork Farms offer an extensive range of cooked meats, pre-packed and in whole joints for your grocer to slice to order. There are hams, roast pork and beef, turkey (smoked and roasted) and roast chicken.

PORK PIES

A wide range of traditionally made, prize winning pies — different to most manufactured pies, as Pork Farms use only a mixture of spiced, fresh, and not cured, pork. The pastry too is quite delicious made as it is to a secret recipe.

SAUSAGES

Pork Farms make their full selection of pork and beef sausages, some to recipes going back for generations of Nottingham's traditional sausage and pie making family, the Parrs.

BACON

Pork Farms pre-pack their mild Honeydew cured bacon in the range of cuts from prime back to streaky.

MORE TRADITIONAL FARE

Pork Farms believe their traditional meat products range would not be complete without scotch eggs, prize winning black puddings, sausage rolls, liver sausage, haslet, polony and faggots.

HOT EATING PIES & PASTIES

Traditional baking of secret recipes again go to make the Pork Farms range of eating pies and Cornish pasties with their rich meat fillings.

ABOVE: *Pork Farms shop, High Street, Beeston, Nottingham c. 1960.*

PREVIOUS PAGE (LEFT) AND RIGHT: *In 1972, shortly after the opening of the new Pork Farms' Queen's Drive facility, a Nottingham Evening Post reporter and photographer visited the site. These pictures were part of the 1972 Nottingham Evening Post article.*

PREVIOUS PAGE (RIGHT): *A Pork Farms product brochure from the archive.*

During the years since he bought the business in 1947, Ken Parr had built up Pork Farms from the original two backstreet shops to a large manufacturing concern with 15 retail outlets. TN Parr and Pork Farms shared a state of intense, ever-increasing competition. Both firms operated on similar lines and were engaged in duplicate operations. The similarity was emphasised by the fact that Ken had learned his trade at TN Parr and was making an identical range of products by identical methods. TN Parr's products, especially its sausages, had long been well-known for quality and flavour and the firm had always made a first-rate pork pie. Frank Samworth, however, would have been the first to acknowledge that a Pork Farms pie had the edge over Parr's. Increasingly Frank Samworth and his sons, with business growth in mind, felt that Pork Farms could be an extremely suitable acquisition for the business.

In 1965 Frank Samworth telephoned Ken Parr with the suggestion that Pork Farms and TN Parr would do well to merge. However as much as this proposition interested him, Ken was obliged to reply that he had been contacted the previous day by Garfield Weston of Associated British Foods (ABF) and offered £400,000 in straight cash for the business. So, for the time, that was that — although in the event, this reunion of the two Parr businesses was only delayed.

But by 1967, ABF was having second thoughts about its meat group having been unable to make any worthwhile money from it. David Samworth approached ABF with a proposition to buy Pork Farms but was rebuffed. Then in 1969, ABF also learned that the Corporation of Nottingham had decided to build a large housing development and that a compulsory purchase order was a direct threat to all Pork Farms' manufacturing units! At this point David Samworth approached ABF with another offer to buy Pork Farms. This was refused, as were all the subsequent offers that were made on an almost daily basis. It soon became clear that the ultimate decision lay with Garfield Weston and his son Gary, with whom David made an appointment.

The only venue that could be managed was at Blackpool over breakfast, and the meeting was attended by Frank Samworth Senior and David. Gary Weston opened the proceedings by expressing his dissatisfaction with Pork Farms saying: 'This firm is always offering me pie

yesterday and pie tomorrow but I want some pie today!' The negotiations were difficult but the outcome was that the Samworths agreed to buy Pork Farms for £510,000, to be paid at the rate of one-third down and one-third a year over the following two years.

On the completion of this transaction Frank Samworth retired from all executive business and David was asked by him and his brothers to take over as Chairman and Managing Director of TN Parr. To this he agreed and Frank Senior formally retired as Chairman and handed all his shares in the company to his sons. He then accepted an invitation to become Honorary Life President of the company and remained on the board as a Non-Executive Director.

Many a small family business grows big under the direction of its founder and then fails because the founder hangs on to power and cannot accede to new ideas and plans. But, although Frank Samworth had no personal experience in running a large organisation, he knew intuitively where the firm was going; he also knew that times had changed and that modern methods were essential if the company was to fulfil his early hopes of achieving a leading position in the food industry.

While negotiating the purchase of Pork Farms, David Samworth had been offered what was described to him as a 'very nice little bakery business' in Stoke on Trent called William Watson Ltd. David could see two purposes in the purchase of Watsons: it would provide sufficient production space to cope with the expansion planned for Pork Farms; and its van sales organisation would complement and widen that of TN Parr.

This transaction, however, presented a serious difficulty. The price agreed upon was £150,000 that, added to the first instalment of the cost of acquiring Pork Farms, amounted to £320,000; in addition, some reserve capital was essential for the ongoing expenditure required to rationalise both acquisitions. All this amounted to far more than the family could raise from their bank, so David, determined not to go back on the Watsons deal, set about finding the money in the City.

After an outright refusal from City merchant bankers, Singer & Friedlander, David then approached the firm's own bankers, Midland, for money but he was refused due to the bank lending restrictions in place at the time. Valuing the Samworth relationship, Midland suggested he contact the merchant bankers Samuel Montagu & Company,

with whom it had close connections. After a hurried telephone introduction, David went straight to the offices of Samuel Montagu and in David's own words: 'within a couple of hours I walked out with a half-million facility'. During this decisive meeting Samuel Montagu also agreed to handle the flotation of the Samworth group if the time ever came.

The purchase of Pork Farms had, through necessity, been completed without reference to Ken Parr and he was astonished when David Samworth telephoned and asked him to join the board, which he agreed to do. With the merger completed, David and John took over control of Pork Farms while Frank Junior stayed on to manage TN Parr.

The merger with Pork Farms doubled the Samworth business almost overnight. With Pork Farms came 22 retail outlets, many on prime

sites where Parr's was not represented, and 24 wholesale delivery vans. Combined, the two firms had 1,000 employees, 49 shops and 58 vans. One immediate benefit of the amalgamation was that it established the combination of skills and knowledge to make and promote nationally branded products. And at long last the Samworths were able to fulfil the ambition of marketing what could be described as 'the Best Pork Pie in England' — a boast that was indisputable.

ABOVE: *A Pork Farms shop and van in Nottingham in the 1970s.*

It was a part of the Samworth/ABF Weston deal that Pork Farms' senior management would stay with the Samworths and it was on this basis that Pork Farms' Managing Director, Bryan Skelston, joined the Samworth business.

He subsequently became a member of Pork Farms' main board and Managing Director of the Pork Farms brand — a position he retained until 1978. He worked well with the Samworth brothers and in time became their trusted business colleague and friend.

Within weeks of the merger, a start was made on integrating the Pork Farms delivery fleet with TN Parr's van sales. A start was also made on further enlarging the Group's retail chain and by 1970 the Group was running more than 50 shops, some as TN Parr, some as Pork Farms because of the demand for both brands.

An important landmark happened at this time, the development of business with the major grocery multiples. With TN Parr's reputation going before him, David was able to confront buyers for the multiples with a sample product and a simple question: 'We have a super product here. Would you like it under your own label?' David's first 'own label' approach was made to Sainsbury's in 1970 and it resulted in a deal with pork pies which over the years built up into very big business and established outlets for Parr's products all over the UK. This marked the launch of an increasingly important aspect of the Samworth business from the 1970s to today.

The late 1960 and early 1970s were momentous for personal reasons as well for the Samworth family, for it was at this time that David met and married his wife Rosemary. They had first met at the opening meet of the Cottesmore hunt in 1968; courted during the season and were engaged by the time of the closing meet. Four children followed, the eldest, Mark — whom we shall meet later on — born in 1970, Mary in 1972, Susannah in 1975, and Victoria in 1977. John Samworth too met his wife to be, Lesley, in this period — in fact, at the 1971 TN Parr staff Christmas party. She and John were married in 1976.

By 1970 the family owned 50 retail outlets and was operating 80 wholesale van sales rounds. Turnover was £4 million and pre-tax profits exceeded £100,000 per annum — figures that implied that the Samworth family was very wealthy. But this wealth was only on paper,

"THIS LITTLE PIGGY WENT TO MARKET."

ABOVE: *Pork Farms goes public (from the* Daily Express, *November 1971).*

for in fact no member of the family possessed any financial security and certainly very little ready cash. It therefore seemed that, in 1971, the time had arrived to 'go public' — that is, to float the group on the Stock Exchange.

From the entrepreneur's point of view there are usually great advantages in selling a self-created company to the public for cash. Such a course brings ready money for the proprietor's own use or to reinvest elsewhere. Further, if the proprietor retains management of the company he has an incentive to stimulate the business for the benefit his own shareholdings — as well as that of others.

LEFT: *Pork Farms delivery vans, Queen's Drive, Nottingham, 1972.*

The bankers Samuel Montagu, which had put up the required money at the time of the Pork Farms merger, agreed to handle the flotation. The parent company at the time was TN Parr Limited and Pork Farms was one of its subsidiaries. But in order to retain the fame of the brand name, the names were switched and the company went public as Pork Farms plc. Only 35 per cent of the ordinary shares were to be offered to the public, with the family retaining 65 per cent.

On completion of the flotation, a new board of directors, which differed very little from the old, was formed — that is, Frank Samworth

Senior remained as President, David was Chairman and Managing Director. The remainder of the board comprised John and Frank Samworth and Ken Parr.

For some months prior to the flotation, David Samworth had made a point of talking to almost everyone he knew who owned a business to persuade them to sell that business to TN Parr. One of these approaches had been to Ernest Gunner, who owned a large chain of butchers' shops in London and a meat products firm called Holetch Holdings, which he had decided to sell.

Holetch's pre-tax profits for 1971 were £326,000, and the firm's assets (land, buildings, plant and stocks) were valued at £835,000. On this basis Holetch was purchased in 1972 for approximately £2 million, to be paid in instalments spread over eight years. When the purchase was agreed Ernest Gunner joined the board of Pork Farms.

The first annual report of Pork Farms as a public company showed annual turnover of £5.2 million and a profit of £424,100 — and this had evolved from the company purchased by Frank Samworth 22 years previously for £30,000. The key to this success was summed up in David Samworth's statement at the company's first annual meeting:

"It has always been the policy of my brothers Frank and John and myself to use the yardstick of earnings per share as the measurement of our success, realising that by resisting maximisation in the short term, we could sustain greater growth in the long term, hence our investment in modern assets and most particularly management training. We have attempted this growth by staying very much in the meat industry, but moving away from the sale of pork and bacon, which 15 years ago contributed the majority of our sales and profits, and devoting more energy to the sales of branded meat products of a high quality and freshness. We are aware that we are operating in a constantly changing environment and it will be our endeavour in the future to continue the growth in our earnings per share consistent with our aim of improving conditions of employment of all employees, without whom there can be no earnings."

1972 was indeed an eventful year because as soon as the flotation had been completed, the long threatened compulsory purchase order on Pork Farms' Alfred Street premises was put into execution. The

ABOVE: *Pork Farms, Queen's Drive, Nottingham 1985.*

problem was dealt with by starting work on the planning and construction of a large modern bakery on the Lenton Industrial Estate at Queen's Drive, Nottingham. Costing some £700,000, the new plant had facilities to more than double Pork Farms' production and was equipped throughout with 'state of the art' machinery, capable of baking over 3,000 pies an hour.

By 1972 Pork Farms was doing good business with the growing supermarket industry, particularly in supplying Sainsbury's with pork pies. Sainsbury's then asked Pork Farms to supply a number of hot-eating products such as steak pies, steak-and-kidney pies and sausage rolls. This was a surprise request and a new large unit (Pork Farms, Trentham) was urgently required to devote to Sainsbury's requirements. This marked a milestone for the family: its first dedicated investment behind own label foods for the supermarkets, and the development of a business model that would come to dominate Samworth Brothers in the future.

A year on from flotation, David Samworth was able to report results far in excess of the optimistic expectations contained in the flotation prospectus. At £11.3 million, turnover was more than double that of the previous year while pre-tax profits amounted to £776,520.

NOTTINGHAM-based Pork Farms, who employ 2,300 people to produce tons of sausages, cooked meats and pork pies, have been taken over in a bid worth around £23m.

The offer comes from Northern Foods, back on the takeover trail in Nottingham after their defeat in a £13m. bid for Shipstone's.

The directors of Pork Farms, whose families hold 52.68 per cent of ~~shares~~ have pledged to accept Northern's offer, cash.

David Samworth, ~~chairm~~an of Pork Farms, ~~Samworth and Mr. Samworth, and their~~ trusts, are retaining a million shares in ~~North~~ern as an invest~~ment~~

~~Pork~~ Farms year end to ~~Febr~~uary this year is ~~expe~~cted to show a pre-tax ~~profi~~t of £2.9m. compared ~~with~~ £1.95m. for the previous 12 months.

Employees

Mr. Nicholas Horsley, ~~cha~~irman of Northern, ~~said~~: "There is no way ~~this~~ deal will not go ~~throu~~gh. I must stre~~ss~~ ~~all~~ ~~job~~...

NORTHERN FOODS—PORK FARMS

'A £23m. offer we could not refuse'

BY JAMES BARTHOLOMEW AND CHRISTOPHER PARKES

A BALANCED diet is as ~~heal~~thy for the body commercial ~~as it~~ is for the human organism ~~It sta~~nds to reason that the de~~velop~~ment of Northern Foods, ~~the~~ takeover of Pork Farms ~~was a~~nnounced yesterday, should ~~be vig~~orous indeed.

~~Nor~~thern Foods, which has ~~grown~~ to its present stature ~~based~~ on dairy and bakery pro~~ducts—~~now has a good plateful ~~of mea~~t—and gravy—before it. ~~Pork F~~arms' pre-tax profits fore~~cast for~~ last year is £2.9m., com~~pared w~~ith £1.95m. in 1976 and ~~£1.1m.~~ in 1973.

~~Born~~ in 1950 from the three ~~local~~ pork butchers' and pie ~~firms ru~~n by Mr. Frank Sam~~worth, it~~s £15,000.

~~Mr. Da~~vid Samworth, chair~~man of Po~~rk Farms, is convinced ~~that~~ at this family business ~~is go~~ing to be gobbled up ~~soon~~ed by the bigger com~~panies~~

~~And~~ he has been waiting ~~for the~~ moment. In March, ~~after ano~~her round in a long ~~run of tak~~eover rumours, Mr. ~~S was~~ as calm and dismis~~sive: "We~~ are just not inter~~est~~ing," he said. Since ~~he ow~~ned 60 per cent of ~~Pork he~~ could afford to be ~~~~

~~He wa~~se reported to be ~~seeking to~~ re Thomas Borth~~wick~~ ~~r~~ecently recovered ~~from it~~s nose pushed out ~~of the~~ tussle for control ~~of the~~ ~~th~~e National Farm~~ers D~~evelopment Trust) ~~w~~hich already has ~~a s~~lice of the pro~~cessed~~ ~~m~~arket through ~~~~

nasty

~~firm~~ to go into ~~the~~ moment. Mr. Samworth ~~said: "I~~ knew I had ~~to sell up~~age." His two ~~children, and ~~as only seven ~~were thus~~

grocers like Fortnum and Mason. The staple income, however, comes from the highly-prized and jealously-guarded chain of store outlets under the prestigious "own brand" labels of companies like Marks and Spencer and J. Sainsbury.

A big advantage in the takeover, for Pork Farms as Mr. Samworth points out, is the possibility of using Northern Food's cash to expand.

But how should a company like Pork Farms develop from here? Mr. Samworth refuses flatly to consider the bacon business— that thorn in the side of the rest of the U.K. meat processing industry. But he sees bright, even brilliant prospects in manufactured meat products.

Pork Farms grew strong on ~~a~~ range of high quality ~~~~ processed meats ~~~~ when consum~~ers~~ meat wa~~s~~ of soar~~ing~~ coincided ~~~~ ing of th~~~~ foods.

In spite ~~~~ pleasant su~~~~ consumers ~~~~ or so by the ~~~~ processors, th~~~~ that the m~~~~ prepared food~~~~ grow. And Po~~~~ there at the star~~~~ daddy of all conv~~~~ the pork pie.

Much is made ~~of~~ tradition of atten~~~~ one of the compan~~y~~ tastings, and Mr. S~~~~ touchingly proud of ~~~~ pany's annual tally ~~~~ blue ribands and oth~~~~ knick-knacks collected ~~~~ competition with oth~~er~~ firms. Last year, for e~~~~ Pork Farms collected mo~~re~~ 50 first prize awards.

Nobody can accuse ~~~~ Samworth of letting Pork F~~~~

asset-rich, claiming to own properties worth £21m. but making pre-tax profits of only £2m.

Northern Foods has made at least 12 takeovers during the seventies. The stockmarket does not normally take kindly to this sort of activity nowadays, but the acquisitions have on the whole, proved successful.

Northern Foods' profits have risen from £5.6m. in 1973 to £17.9m. in 1977 and it is one of the stockbrokers' favourites in the food sector.

Surplus fund~~s~~

Henders~~~~
exam~~~~

£13 MILLION PIE SALE

EXPRESS.

By Ray Heath

A FORTUNE based on pork pies and sausages is soon to be sliced up by a family from Britain's pie town — Melton Mowbray, Leicestershire.

The £13 million is to be paid over to the Samworth family, which yesterday agreed to sell control of their Pork Farms company to Northern Foods, a Hull-based group.

The total value of the bid is £23 million, but the company is largely controlled by ~~chairman~~ Mr David Sam-

worth, other family directors and their families.

Together they have 53 per cent of the shares in Pork Farms, which under the terms of the takeover bid were last night worth £13 million.

Burden

Mr David Samworth, of Thorpe Satchville, Melton Mowbray, said one of the reasons for selling was the possible tax burden he and his family would eventually have to bear if they remained in control of the company.

Mr Samworth is joi~~ning the~~ board of Norther~~n~~ which owns the Hull ~~Br~~ Fox Biscuits and Park~~~~ Bakery.

He is among the ~~~~ on the Pork Farm~~s~~ where his father ~~is~~ president and his ~~brothers~~ Frank and John ~~are~~ directors.

One of the family ~~~~ is a unique form ~~of~~ control.

To make sure ~~Pork~~ Farms produce is ~~up to stan~~dard they all ~~eat a~~ 6 a.m. breakfast o~~f pies~~ and sausages.

EXPANSION AND
THE END OF AN ERA

The Pork Farms acquisition and flotation launched a new period of expansion for the business. However the 1970s also produced big challenges with an oil crisis and three-day week. By the end of the decade there were further developments that saw the Samworth Pork Farms era draw to a close.

LEFT: *Press coverage of the Northern Foods offer in the Nottingham Evening Post.*

The Financial Times *report on the Northern Foods takeover of Pork Farms in June 1978. 'Northern Foods', the article reported, 'which has grown to its present stature mainly on bakery and dairy products, now has a good plateful of meat — and gravy — before it.'*

An article in the Daily Express *regarding the Pork Farms sale.*

RIGHT: *Bryan Skelston (centre) with the Pork Farms production team and a selection of Pork Farms trophies.*

1973 marked the opening of a new distribution depot in London and the launch of Pork Farms' products in the London area. It was also the year when Pork Farms won the Melton Mowbray pork pie championship and awards and prizes at every major bakery competition.

That year also saw the retirement of Frank Samworth Junior from executive duties in the family business. For some time he had taken a diminishing role in the company's administration but had continued to supervise research and development of the products and the maintenance of product quality. During his time with the company, turnover had increased from £250,000 to over £15 million.

One of the reasons behind the business's rising turnover in the face of increasing recession was the growth in demand for pre-cooked and 'convenience foods' — which included cooked meats. It was therefore decided to expand this side of the business through the purchase of Baron Meats, a maker of a variety of cooked meats and turkey-based products which were then probably the best of their kind in the UK.

However the period 1973-76 was a difficult one in many respects, starting as it did with the oil crisis and the three-day week. In 1974 David had warned that the then prevailing low price of pig meat meant future trouble for the industry. In 1975 he was proved right when the price of pork reached a record high level.

During this very troublesome period the price of Pork Farms shares dropped to 60p. But even then, in a statement in 1975, David Samworth was able to report that turnover was up from £15 million to £19 million with a 20 per cent rise of pre-tax profits to £1,244,000. These figures showed that, despite the severity of trading conditions, the Group's profits had almost trebled since the flotation. At this news Pork Farms' shares returned immediately to their flotation price of 115p.

In 1974 a new bakery was built at Beeston to service a new contract to exclusively supply Marks & Spencer with pork pies.

The year 1975-76 proved to be the most difficult in the company's history. There were severe losses through competition from subsidised imports: costs continued to rise even more rapidly than before and government controls still limited the amount by which prices could

Pork Farms Limited 1976 Report to Employees

A message from the Chairman

David Samworth

This is the first occasion on which I have produced a report specifically for everyone who works for Pork Farms. The figures are based on information contained in the formal accounts, and are intended to give in an easily readable form those parts of the accounts which are of particular interest to us all at this present time.

The most important single fact is that, for the first time in ten years, our Company profits are lower than those of the previous year. Profits before tax fell from £1,244,000 to £1,077,000, yet our sales were up by £2,349,000. As you will see from the chart overleaf, with inflation running at 23% per annum, we needed to earn about £1,530,000 in order to stand still.

Because we earned less than that figure, we were unable to retain in the business, for necessary future replacement of machinery and motor vehicles, etc., as much as had been possible in the previous year, and this at a time when inflation was running at record levels.

The reason our profits fell in spite of higher turnover is that our costs rose more rapidly than ever before. At the same time Government price controls limited the amount by which prices could be raised, and thereby prevented us from passing on to our customers more of the increased costs. So our profits fell.

However, whilst profits are a condition of survival, they are also an important factor in the morale of a business, and this extends throughout the whole Organisation. Nothing encourages inefficiency and apathy more quickly than a business that is constantly losing money. A competitive firm can only be successful when the products, or services it provides, are wanted and appreciated by those who are going to buy them, and are priced at a level which gives an adequate return to all concerned.

Whilst true prosperity for us depends to a large extent on the prosperity of the Nation as a whole, each one of us has his, or her, contribution to make in improving productivity and efficiency, for the ultimate benefit of ourselves and our families. That, I am convinced, is the right way ahead for Pork Farms.

May 1976

be raised. Although group turnover for the year increased by £2.4 million to a record £21.7 million, pre-tax profits fell to £1.07 million. At this rate, with inflation running at a record 23 per cent per annum, the company needed to earn some £1.5 million a year in order to stand still. Yet, despite this erosion of profit margins, the company refused to compromise in the quality of its products; this was maintained and, wherever possible, improved — a fact demonstrated in 1977 by Pork Farms winning over 50 prizes in food shows up and down the country. John Samworth put this commitment to quality in very personal terms: "We've always paid great attention to the service that we give, and we've always taken a personal interest in the products. We never go to shops or bakeries without sampling the products, and if there's been any deterioration in quality, we take action to put it right."

ABOVE: *Presentation of a Pork Farms pie to the Lord Mayor of Nottingham, 1978. Left to right: Eddy Edwards, (Development Chef), Wally Huckle, the Lady Mayoress, Bryan Skelston, the Lord Mayor, Reg Gardiner (Retail Supervisor), Allan Pepper (Development Chef).*

During the following year, further steps were taken to increase manufacturing capacity, and van selling operations were enlarged by the addition of many new journeys. These measures eventually resulted in a turn for the better with sales for 1977 rising to £27.25 million, and an 81 per cent improvement in pre-tax profits to a record £1.95 million. The recovery continued throughout 1978 when profits reached a further record of £3.01 million on a turnover of £33.07 million. Throughout these good but trying times, the Samworth family had begun to find itself in a quandary. At the time the brothers owned 65 per cent of Pork Farms' equity in equal shares but they had grown somewhat weary of being on the public company treadmill, of being under the annual scrutiny of shareholders and being expected to increase profits and earnings per share every year. Neither John nor his brother Frank had children, so for them there was no succession to consider, and thus no long-term future for them in Pork Farms. They had worked hard for the business for many years and had no desire to continue working indefinitely for outside interests. They wanted to

sell out, and to do so it was necessary for their shares to have an asset value. Furthermore, the cash from such a sale could be used to expand the family's interests. David, on the other hand, was reluctant to sell Pork Farms but he realised the importance of acting in concert with his brothers. All this, together with many other factors, meant that the brothers decided to team up on this important issue and it so came about they eventually agreed that it was time to sell Pork Farms.

Since its introduction to the market only seven years previously, Pork Farms' pre-tax profits had grown from £424,000 to over £3 million — an achievement that would attract any acquisition-seeking group. David Samworth himself knew of a number of concerns interested in taking over. But the family was determined that Pork Farms was not going to be gobbled up and digested by any big company; they were resolved that it would go to a smaller group — preferably one personally known to the family and, most importantly, one that had a good record regarding its employees. The Samworths did know of such a firm. This was Northern Foods with which David had already had some

ABOVE: *David Samworth with the Queen Mother at the British Meat Festival in 1982.*

contact. The brothers knew and liked a number of Northern Foods' people — and, more important, they knew Northern's good reputation for looking after its people. They were also aware there was an interest from Northern in the Samworth business. In March 1977, David met the board of Northern Foods with a prepared presentation that suggested a price of 500-550p a share. But with Pork Farms' share price then standing at 175p, David was told that Pork Farms was worth only half what he was asking. This eliminated any immediate possibility of compromise or bargaining and ended a most disappointing meeting.

It was at this point that John Samworth resigned his place on the board of Pork Farms after 24 active years with the business — the last seven years of which he had spent as a 'roving director' across the business.

That year, due to changes in the company structure, the company was able to increase its dividend significantly and its shares immediately rose from 130p to 325p. There matters stood until April 1978 when, with rumours of a possible takeover, Pork Farms' shares rose to 460p

— that is, the price had trebled since 1976. At that Nicholas Horsley, chairman of Northern Foods, telephoned David Samworth to say that Northern Foods was now willing to buy at 550p per share. This was the price that David had asked a year previously, and so now he could afford to increase it. After extensive negotiations Northern Foods agreed to offer 675p in cash payable with four Northern shares (then valued at 90p) plus 315p in cash.

The total purchase price then amounted to £23 million which was a full 16 times the estimated pre-tax profits for 1977-78. Considering also that Pork Farms' net tangible assets in the 1977 balance sheet were only £2.7 million, this was an excellent price, and on 6 June 1978 David was able to issue the Pork Farms board's recommendation to its shareholders to accept the offer. Thus the group of companies built upon the small local business founded by George Samworth over a century before finally passed out of the family's hands.

Pork Farms was no longer a Samworth-owned business, but the family's involvement with the firm continued, with David Samworth as its Chairman. David was also kept busy with other activities. In 1980 he was asked to chair the Government's Meat and Livestock Commission which had been formed in 1967 to improve the marketing of meat and livestock in the UK. He accepted this invitation and stayed with the Commission for four years.

John Samworth retired from the board of Pork Farms in 1977 and in March 1981 David finally resigned the chairmanship of the company and his directorship of Northern Foods, thus breaking the last Samworth link with Pork Farms and TN Parr. It was with mixed feelings that he left Queen's Drive for the last time.

During the following year David was invited to become a Non-Executive Director of Imperial Group, then one of the largest companies in the UK and then, in 1984, took on a full-time executive role. He was also a council member of 'Food from Britain', during this period. In July 1984 he was recommended to become a Deputy Lieutenant of the County of Leicestershire, and in the quaint wording used by tradition, Her Majesty the Queen 'did not disapprove'. Then, in the New Year Honours List for 1985, David was awarded the CBE for his work with the Meat and Livestock Commission.

THIS PAGE: *John Samworth at Ginsters in 1977.*

OPPOSITE: *The new Charnwood site in the late 1980s.*

A FRESH START

The purchase of a Cornish pasty business that had started life in a converted egg packing factory marked the start of the next chapter in the Samworth story. Soon a second business, Walker & Son also joined the fold.

Ginsters was founded by Cornish dairy farmer Geoffrey Ginster with his two sons Gerald and Barry. In 1967 the Ginster family started to buy in fresh pies and pasties to sell from vans to various local retail outlets. The holiday season in Cornwall was good for four and a half months of the year during which time hundreds of thousands of people visited Cornwall and they wanted to sample Cornish pasties. The appeal of the pasty to holiday makers was such that on returning to their homes they started to demand them from their local shopkeepers and in time the pasty became almost as popular as the pork pie.

It was to satisfy this large and growing market that the Ginsters decided to make their own Cornish pasties. They started the business in a near-derelict egg-packing station covering some 8,000 square feet in the small town of Callington, in East Cornwall. After major renovations to the building they installed a couple of food mixers, a vegetable dicer,

a conveyor belt and two large ovens. Then, in August 1969, with a staff of four, Geoffrey Ginster started production of a first-class pasty from a 'secret recipe' he claimed to have obtained from a ship's cook. His initial target was 20,000 units a week and on the first day two dozen were produced. By 1977 the firm employed 50 people and was making an annual profit of £200,000 on a turnover of £1 million. Geoffrey Ginster began thinking of selling the business and retiring. John and David Samworth, having observed the development of the business over the preceding few years from a distance, saw that the firm's success could go much further.

With the sale of Pork Farms looming, John Samworth met with Geoffrey Ginster and made an offer for the business in a private capacity — which necessitated John's resignation from the Pork Farms board. The offer was accepted in principle and subsequent negotiations were conducted by John in consultation with the rest of the family. The final price agreed upon was £1 million in cash. The overall shareholding position was that one third of Ginsters was owned by Frank Samworth

The Cornish pasty is a snack food that has its roots in the Cornish tin mining industry. Miners would take their dinner to work in the form of a pastry case filled with meat and vegetables and sealed with a large crimp, which provided a handle for the miner to hold while eating his pasty. In those days, the crimp would be discarded; now, as few people eat their pasty underground, it tends to be eaten!

ABOVE: *John Stephenson and Eric Holdship inspecting Cornish pasty production at Ginsters Lynher Bakery, 1987.*

Junior, a third by John and a third by David's family trust. All three Ginsters agreed to stay on with the firm; Geoffrey as company consultant, Gerald and Barry as joint Managing Directors. Space was already very scarce at the plant and in 1978 a government funded factory standing next to the existing site was acquired. This was named Tamar Bakery, after the nearby River Tamar. It was equipped with modern baking and packing facilities and when it was completed the old unit was refitted to prepare pasty fillings. John Samworth had spent most of his working life on the sales side of food products, and under his

ABOVE: *Making Cornish pasties by hand at Tamar, 1980.*

direction and through his established contacts, deals in Ginsters products were completed with some of the big multiples — Sainsbury's, Tesco, Waitrose and Marks & Spencer. By this time another, hitherto unimportant, market was now coming into its own, although it was one that Ginsters had been watching for some years. This was the servicing of the proliferating garage forecourt shops. In its Cornish pasty sales campaigns, Ginsters had noticed the fast-growing demand for handy foods, suitable for eating on the move — for which the Cornish pasty is ideal. Ginsters designed a range of suitable 'eating-on-the-move'

snacks. Then, because independent retailers are often restricted for store space, the firm provided over 3,000 retailers with the 'Ginsters Food Bar' — a refrigerated unit with a digital thermometer for precise temperature control, fitted with a small microwave oven for products that customers might want heated. One of the many advantages of this method of selling is that the products are attractively displayed all over the country in the same way.

David Samworth's departure from Imperial Group in 1984 coincided with John's desire to reduce his day to day involvement with the Ginsters business. John therefore relinquished the Ginsters' chairmanship to his brother, and David threw himself into the development of the business. When David joined Ginsters at Callington, a staff of 350

ABOVE: *Left to right, Bryan Skelston, Godfrey Tucker, Denis Kearney, David Samworth, John Samworth and Chris Edwards at the Tamar Bakery.*

people was working round the clock to fulfil the increasing demand. Production was running at over a million units a week with sales extending virtually the length and breadth of the British Isles — and all goods were delivered within 24 hours of baking. In November 1985 the name of the Ginsters holding company was changed from Gorran Foods to Samworth Brothers, with the main purpose of the name-change being to reflect the personal involvement of David and John Samworth in the affairs of the company. The Samworths had a family business once more — and a big one, for during that year Ginsters sales reached £14.2 million with pre-tax profits of £1.7 million. In order to meet estimated future requirements it was decided to initiate a massive investment plan to double potential production. Ginsters announced in August 1986 that, at a cost of some £3.5 million, a new bakery would be built alongside Tamar Bakery, on the site of the egg-packing

BELOW: Frederick Sewell Wright, who worked at Walkers from the age of 14 to retirement with a break during World War II, when he joined the 8th Army c. 1938-9.

station where the company had started 17 years before. The new bakery, named Lynher (after the River Lynher), was finished and commissioned in the spring of 1987. Although the new plant was to be sited in close proximity to the old, it was intended that the two factories would be run as independent units, each with its own production and profit targets. The opening of Lynher bakery created 130 new jobs, but by the time it was in operation, demand had already overtaken the event and, within a year, a 4,000 square feet extension had to be added.

1986 also marked the start of a new chapter in the Midlands with the acquisition of Walker & Son of Leicester. Walkers was established in 1820 by a Mansfield pork butcher, Mark Walker, who came to Leicester with his son, Henry James Walker, to open a butcher's shop in Leicester High Street. On outgrowing the High Street shop at

BELOW: *A Walker & Son archive shot of the Oxford Street bakery in Leicester in c. 1920.*

the turn of the century, the firm moved to larger and better premises in Cheapside, which, in time, became Leicester's best known pork butcher's. In common with all butchers, Walkers suffered badly during World War II and the business diversified into potato crisps. At first the crisps were sold only in the Walkers shops; then, after an agreement with Everards the local brewery, they were displayed in many local public houses. When meat was finally de-rationed in 1954, production of Walkers' traditional foods began to return to normal. But crisp production had grown to become a major part of Walkers' business. In the years between 1962 and 1970 sales of Walkers crisps trebled until, by 1970, they had captured 34 per cent of the UK crisp market. In 1971 the American firm, Standard Brands made an offer for Walkers crisps and the business was sold for £3 million. (The still successful Walkers crisp brand is now owned by PepsiCo). The disposal of the crisp business meant that Walkers' sales and cashflow were greatly reduced, and despite all efforts to re-establish its traditional business in a new bakery in Cobden Street, turnover and profits continued to decrease over the years. With dwindling profits and an uncertain outlook, the Walker family decided to put the firm up for sale and the company was purchased by Samworth Brothers in 1986 for £1,750,000. The existing Walkers board was disbanded and a new one formed with John Samworth as chairman and Bryan Skelston, previously Managing Director of the Pork Farms brand, as Vice-Chairman and Managing Director. With the acquisition completed, Bryan Skelston was given the task of rationalising Walkers management and manufacturing procedures. Over the following five years the Cobden Street premises were enlarged and fully refurbished to provide a 10,000 square feet facility for cooked meats, ham and bacon. Pie and sausage manufacturing methods were much improved and the management system overhauled. On the retail side four of the 12 Walkers shops were closed and the others refurbished. By 1988 Walkers was showing a profit double that achieved in any previous year. Much credit for this must go to Bryan Skelston and his management team consisting of Sales Director, John Cox, Production Director Peter Harris and Finance Director Geoff Aldwinckle. Together, they increased sales from £3 million to £30 million. In 1987 Walkers' production base was extended with the acquisition of a neighbouring unit on the Cobden Street estate. Over the following years, unit after unit was occupied one after the other until, today, only two units are not under the Samworth flag. Under Samworth Brothers management, Walkers' market penetration also reached a state of continual expansion and, in 1988, plans were put in hand for an ambitious new venture in Leicester. At this time Walkers was producing an average of 35 tons of pork pies a week. In its own shops alone, some 25 tons were sold during the 1988 Christmas shopping period. The old Cobden Street works, now covering 9,000 square feet, was operating round-the-clock shifts to keep up with the

BELOW: David Samworth with Brian Stein displaying the 1996-1997 Business of the Year Award, together with the best Sales and Marketing Campaign Award.

RIGHT: *Master baker Ian Heircock and some of his haul of championship pie prizes.*

increasing orders and no amount of expansion there would have made it possible to meet all demands — let alone to produce the quantities aimed for in the long term. Further expansion was a priority and plans were put in hand to build a new bakery at Beaumont Leys in Leicester which would multiply the Cobden Street output. Named Charnwood Bakery, it was designed to increase the total pie production from 35 tons to 140 tons — a million pies a week! Built on a pleasant five-and-a-half acre greenfield site at a cost of £7 million, the 50,000 square foot bakery was capable of meeting all Walkers' short and long term needs. The greatly increased production facilities at Charnwood enabled the Walkers range to be extended. It included an assortment of pork pies, hot-eating pies, pasties, quiches and sausage rolls — a range which became so broad that Walkers was able to boast (unofficially) that it could provide anything a customer could want — provided that it was wrapped in pastry.

With the new Tamar, Lynher and Charnwood bakeries developing fast and Ginsters becoming a nationwide brand, the business was entering another expansive phase.

DEVELOPING CULTURE AND MANAGEMENT

With the foundations of the business laid and an ambitious growth plan in place, attention turned to management structure and the shaping of company culture.

From the acquisition of Walkers in 1986, the Samworth family once again owned a business with multiple operations on different sites. With ambitions to grow both the Walkers and Ginsters businesses way beyond their then size, it became clear that a more structured form of management, and a clearer understanding of the Samworth Brothers culture, would be important.

So in 1986 the industrial consultant Professor Charles Handy was called in to carry out a detailed investigation of the company's operations. Handy, a former Shell executive and later professor at the London Business School, was a well-known writer and broadcaster on business affairs, and consultant to many organisations in business, government and the voluntary sector. The objective of Professor Handy's exercise was set out at the time as three bullet points:

• To find ways to make Samworth Brothers into one of the most interesting and worthwhile companies to work for in Britain so that the Group will attract more of the best recruits.

• That this would make the company more effective and more efficient and thus more profitable.

• That people will be proud to work for the company and will be better off.

PREVIOUS PAGE (LEFT): *The 1997 Holdings Board. Back row, left to right, Chris Edwards, Brian Stein and Mark Samworth, front row, left to right, Jonathan Warburton, David Samworth and Nick Linney.*

PREVIOUS PAGE (RIGHT): *Sir Ian (now Lord) MacLaurin, then Chairman of Tesco with Peter Harris (left) and Dennis Lock (right) on his visit to Charnwood Bakery in 1994.*

BELOW: *Massey Ferguson Award Ceremony 1996. Left to right, Susannah Samworth, David Samworth CBE DL (Recipient of the 1996 Award), Rosemary Samworth, Victoria Samworth, Mark Samworth.*

ABOVE: *In 1994 David and Mark Samworth attended the 'Leading the Family Business' course at the IMD in Lausanne, Switzerland. At the time the course was one of only two programmes aimed at improving the management and governance of family businesses. David and Mark gained access to the latest thinking in a field that was at the time ignored by most business researchers and advisors. The course material was supplemented by the experience of delegates, who included future Samworth Brothers Non-Executive Director and Chairman Nick Linney. Pictured, top row, second right, David Samworth. Middle row, third left, Mark Samworth; centre, Nick Linney; sixth right, Miles Linney.*

After some discussion, Professor Handy put a number of proposals to the Board. They were that:

1. The style of management throughout the company should be based on delegated responsibility and trust, and that appropriate training and education should be given to fit people for those responsibilities.
2. The personnel and remuneration policies should be the best that the company could afford, and built on the premise that any increase in added value should go to the workers as well as the management, either in cash or in the form of improved conditions and opportunities.
3. The structures of the company should facilitate communication and discussion about the company's affairs with opportunities for the workforce to influence their own work and destinies.
4. To achieve these aims, Professor Handy suggested that a small team of key people should be formed from all levels of the company to visit (in pairs) a number of showcase companies in different fields to give them an idea of what is possible.

Professor Handy's proposals were accepted unreservedly and implemented. The team made a number of recommendations to the Board

to improve training, communications, working conditions, benefits package and continuous improvement. The Board approved the implementation of these developments and David Samworth issued a policy statement of the Board's beliefs:

"We believe that our most important asset is our people. Every individual will be accorded dignity and respect at all times, and be given every opportunity to develop to their maximum potential. Our customers play a vital role in ensuring our continued success, and we will always give them the best possible service and attention. The company will strive for excellence in all that it does."

This exercise helped the family make a start in defining a management structure and approach that could carry the Group forward. In the early 1990s, though, as Samworth Brothers continued to grow, it became clear that a longer-term strategy needed to be developed. Looking around for a consultant to work with, the company engaged Alex Knight, then head of Ashridge Consulting — a decision that has

ABOVE: *Retirement of Denis Kearney, Hambleton Hall, October 1997. Left to right, Mark Samworth, David Samworth, Denis Kearney, Brian Stein, John Samworth, Chris Edwards, Jonathon Warburton, Nick Linney.*

served both parties well, as Knight continues to work with Samworth Brothers more than 20 years later.

Samworth Brothers' work with Alex Knight in the early 1990s resulted in the complete revamping of the Group's executive management structure. In January 1996, a new parent company was formed to encompass all of the Group's activities, and provide public limited company (PLC) levels of accountability and corporate governance. Samworth Brothers (Holdings) Limited, known as the Holdings Board, chaired by David Samworth and with two external Non-Executive Directors — Nick Linney of the Mansfield firm of printers and publishers, W&J Linney, and Jonathan Warburton of Warburtons Bakers — in compliance with the suggestions made by Sir Adrian Cadbury's report on corporate governance. A third Non-Executive, Dr Leslie Atkinson, joined the Board in December 1999, having held senior positions in BP. In accordance with the policy that the group should be run to the

LEFT: *Brian Stein bacame Group Managing Director of Samworth Brothers in April 1997.*

same standards as a PLC, the Holdings Board has always incorporated an audit committee and a remuneration and development committee.

Under the Holdings Board, the reorganisation saw the creation of the Group Executive Board, which still oversees the day-to-day management of the company. Also chaired, at the time, by David Samworth, this original Board included then Finance Director Chris Edwards, Ginsters Managing Director Denis Kearney, Mark Samworth and Brian Stein. Having been known to the Samworth management for many years, Brian Stein came to Samworth Brothers in 1995 from Northern Foods where he had been a senior director running a large section of Northern's meat group. He joined Samworth Brothers as Managing

BELOW: *Family friends and colleagues celebrate David Samworth's 65th birthday at Chetwode House.*

Director of the Charnwood Bakery, and went straight onto the Group Executive Board. With this reorganisation completed, David began a process of gradually handing over the chairmanship of all the Group's subsidiaries. Brian became Group Managing Director in 1997 and Group Chief Executive of Samworth Brothers in 1999. As we shall see, he played a major role in the subsequent success of the group.

Interviewed just after these changes had been instigated, Alex Knight set out the rationale:

"At Ashridge we'd been doing a lot of research on how much value was added to businesses by their head office operations, and found that, more often, large central administration teams actually destroy value. Samworth Brothers was committed to a small head office team, and that forced the adoption of a federalist approach. Each business had its own small board, including only the managing, finance, sales and production directors, as well as a chairman who was on the Group Executive Board, and those individual boards were clearly responsible for delivering a good service to their customers. There was, and is, very little interference from the centre."

There is no doubt that the reforms in management structure instituted in collaboration with Professor Handy in 1986, and later built on by the work carried out by Alex Knight, laid the foundations for the subsequent growth of Samworth Brothers.

The federalist model that Alex Knight alluded to gave significant freedom to the boards of each Samworth Brothers business but, for any decentralised system to work, it requires clearly defined boundaries. A set of guidelines was therefore drawn up to define what federalism meant in practice, so that each board would be aware of the obligations and limits of belonging to Samworth Brothers. After much consultation, five governing principles were defined:

The Delegation of Authority — Responsibility and opportunity is passed to those best placed to affect a good result. Unnecessary interference is avoided, but good results are asked for in return.

Twin Citizenship — Everyone in the business is a member of both their operating company (Bradgate, for example) and Samworth Brothers, and pride in both is encouraged.

Common Language — If a complex group of companies is to be

coordinated effectively without central control, then a common understanding and a common set of definitions is required.

Interdependence — No individual business in the Group exists in isolation. When acting on behalf of the operating company, one must be aware that other companies in the Group might be affected by one's actions.

Separation of Powers — The Group should ensure that good governance and best practice is enshrined in the structure of the business. It is no longer the case that the Chief Executive and the Chairman can be the same person.

ABOVE: *The company's Policy Statement developed at this time not only talked about success being built on 'constant respect for People, Quality and Profit'. It also emphasised the role of high quality facilities and the importance of the site environment, with aspects such as good quality landscaping. This commitment has continued over the years as shown here at Bradgate Bakery.*

In practice, the work started by Professor Handy and continued by Alex Knight allowed the evolution of a structure that was flexible, could accommodate change and growth to an extent, and could motivate and give considerable freedom to the management teams of each business.

The growth and success of the business cannot, of course, be attributed to its structure. David Samworth was also keen to emphasise that Samworth Brothers is more than just a corporation. As he wrote in the company's Policy Statement (personally signed by David and the Managing Director of each Samworth site, and prominently displayed across the Group):

"Our success depends upon our constant respect for People, Quality and Profit.

We believe that our most important asset is our people. Every individual will be treated with dignity and respect at all times, and be given every opportunity to develop to their maximum potential.

We will continuously improve the quality of the facilities for our people, the product and service for our customers, and the partnership with our suppliers.

We earn our profits to reinvest in the future for the benefit of our customers, our people, and the communities in which we work."

The culture of Samworth Brothers was summarised as 'People, Quality, Profit,' or PQP. An annual staff survey was instigated to keep track of whether or not PQP was being practised as well as preached in the sites. (An annual research study still takes place at the time of this new edition in 2015). It was during this period that the Samworth Academy concept was developed. The objective was to allow staff in each of the businesses access to a training facility, known as a Samworth Academy. The Academy helped to ensure that the culture of the business was taught, explained and encouraged across the Group, but in addition staff had access to other life skill training opportunities, everything from learning a language, to improving driving competence or even mastering fly-fishing! All managers attended a presentation in small groups, originally given by David, on the history of the business and how its culture has developed. (Again these sessions continue today, now hosted by Mark Samworth,)

THE CORNWALL JOURNEY

Just a decade after the purchase of Ginsters, the Cornwall businesses were already prospering. However this was just the start of a long and successful era for Cornwall and the emergence of Ginsters as a national brand.

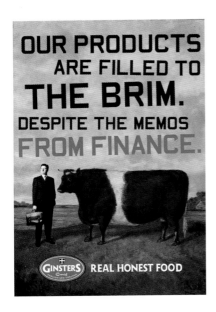

OUR PRODUCTS ARE FILLED TO THE BRIM. DESPITE THE MEMOS FROM FINANCE.

GINSTERS **REAL HONEST FOOD**

ABOVE AND RIGHT: *Brave and thoughtful advertising has helped to evolve the Ginsters name into a national brand.*

ABOVE: *Shaun Galloway, Ginsters' Finance Director, is pictured in this campaign.*

PREVIOUS PAGE (LEFT): *Ginsters' Development Chef, Toby Hill, in the Ginsters development kitchen.*

PREVIOUS PAGE (RIGHT): *The Ginsters 'Feed the Man' advertising series which launched in 2014 has won a number of industry awards.*

Great things had been achieved by Ginsters since it had been purchased in 1977. In 1989 the two Callington sites, with a combined staff of 900, were jointly turning out some two million products a week — which represented an increase in turnover from £1 million in 1978 to £45 million. Eighty vans were supplying 8,800 customers — supermarkets, garage forecourts, snack bars, motorway cafes, clubs and fast food shops. However still bigger ambitions were harboured by Samworth Brothers and the Ginsters management team — to turn Ginsters into a national brand. 1989 saw the ramping up of brand marketing activity to achieve this target.

At the time, the Ginsters brand was still focused solely on Cornish pasties, a market that had become somewhat static and which at that time appealed to only a limited section of the country. The task now was to build the Ginster name into a powerful national brand, to give it identity and a reputation for quality and make it into a name to be equalled with that of Kellogg's or Mars.

So it was decided to branch out further from Cornish pasties into a wider range of similar 'portable' foodstuffs and establish the Ginsters brand name firmly within that demand. These new lines comprised a new range of 'hand-held' products especially designed for the 'on-the-move' market. These included a line marketed as 'Savoury Slices', that is, small sandwich-type snacks with various savoury fillings, which were an easily handled equivalent to a slice of pie; Buffet Bars, comprising a sausage meat casing wrapping a mixture of coleslaw, cheese and mayonnaise; and Scotch eggs. These new lines filled a gap in the field of 'portable' snacks and found a popular niche in the forecourt market.

The Managing Director of Ginsters, Denis Kearney, along with his team of Peter Castell, Brian Kelly, Chris Edwards and Godfrey Tucker, had identified a lucrative market and positioned Ginsters through strong branding and commercial acumen to exploit it. Their work and vision was to create a stepping-stone from which Ginsters would later grow to be one of the most valuable chilled food brands in the UK. However more capacity was needed. Despite a programme of efficiency improvements at Callington, the two bakeries were at 80 per cent of capacity during peak periods, and the potential market with the multiples and van sales highlighted a need for a third bakery. Sited with

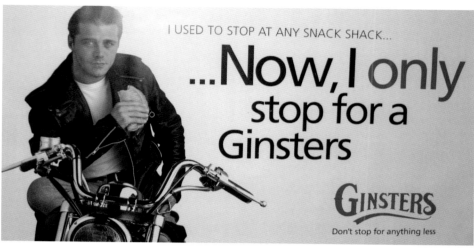

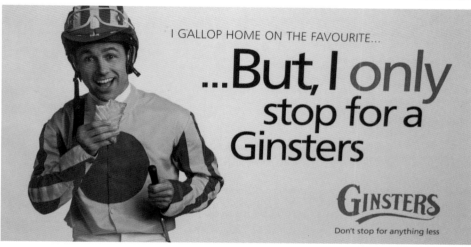

ABOVE: *Van sales have always been a strong aspect of the Ginsters business.*

good access to the motorway system and in an area of plentiful labour, Launceston proved to be an ideal location. Construction began in 1990 and was completed in June 1992. The bakery is set in a pleasing land-scape and is named Kensey — again, after another local river.

The production, baking, chilling and packing facilities at Kensey Bakery were designed to be highly automated and to take the business into the next century. Its total cost was £8 million and it generated 200 new jobs in the area. By the end of 1992 Ginsters had cornered 25 per cent of the £50 million per year Cornish pasty market and, in addition, was making meat and vegetable pies, sausage rolls, quiches, a range of savoury snacks and fruit dessert items.

Since 1992 the Ginsters business has continued to expand, and the brand has become much better known and more successful. Though many of its traditional markets have shrunk recently, total brand turn-over has quadrupled in size. Ginsters has also developed a valuable own label business with Tesco and Marks & Spencer. Continued investment in the brand, initially through press and posters, then radio and now national TV and a very busy social media campaign has seen Ginsters becoming brand leader in every region in the country and featuring highly in *The Grocer* magazine's list of top 100 brands. The brand has also launched its first ever meat snacking range, Ginsters Meat Club, one in a long line of continuing product innovations, and announced a new partnership with the Help for Heroes charity.

ABOVE: *The new Ginsters Meat Club range launched in 2015, another example of Ginsters' continued product innovation.*

SAMWORTH PEOPLE

Ian Worth
Operator, Kensey Foods

Ian Worth, Operator at Kensey Foods, is one of the longest serving members of staff at Samworth Brothers, clocking up nearly 43 years in the Group.

He first started back in 1972 with a part-time role at Ginsters, and through his older brother Phil who also worked there, he soon heard of an opportunity for a full-time job.

He recalls getting on his motorbike and riding in the rain on his first day and people commenting on the state of his hair when he walked into the bakery! It wasn't long though before he had a hat on and was packing pasties.

At Ginsters he did some driving for a while which saw him doing deliveries all over the West Country. However, in 1994 he moved over to work at Kensey Foods, where he has been an Operator ever since.

He has certainly seen some changes at these two bakeries over the years; when he started Ginsters just made one product, a hand-crimped pasty – now it makes over 60 products. At Kensey, when Ian first joined they just made apple pies, while now he is involved making sure a whole range of products are cooked properly, from custard tarts to meringues.

Ian has enjoyed attending the long service events over the years, and remembers meeting Sir David and his brothers when they visited the bakery.

Ian isn't the only member of the Worth family to work for Samworth Brothers, his older brother Phil has now retired as a driver, and his other brother Dave still drives for the Group. Each of their sons also work for the Group; Ian's son Scott at Kensey Foods, Phil's son Richard at Tamar Foods, and Dave's son Gavin in the Callington Fleet Maintenance depot.

Between them the family has worked for over 130 years for Samworth Brothers!

The brand has become highly recognisable, enjoying a loyal consumer following. Sales have grown through the major retailers and into new markets with students, as well as into the rail network and in convenient stores and cafes.

Mark Duddridge, Managing Director of Ginsters for many years and now the Group Executive Board Director with responsibility for Ginsters, is clear on priorities. "Brand development is absolutely key for us," he says. "In the time Ginsters has been owned by Samworth Brothers, it has gone from being a regional to a national brand, and is now over twice the size of our nearest competitor. We're selling our products into a market that is up to 80 per cent own label. Although we're twice the size of the next brand, we have to be aware that brands are only 20 per cent of our market as a whole. So selling into those markets is hard, and the brand has to add value. That's why brand management is high priority for us. There is a recognition at Group Board level that Ginsters has to be treated a little bit differently, that there is huge emotional value to the brand for the business."

ABOVE: A celebration event for the '25 year Club' — for members of staff of the Cornish businesses who have served over 25 years with the company. This event was in 2014.

The Ginsters business has changed considerably in the last ten years. The brand has significantly expanded its customer base, but this growth has primarily been achieved via the major supermarkets. In contrast the brand's traditional roadside business has seen a contraction as forecourts have changed, with coffee chains and retail brands moving into that space.

Production technology has moved forward spectacularly with the

Westward Laboratories

Louis Pasteur once observed that 'it is the microbes which will have the last word'. This has never been the case at Samworth Brothers which has always been noted for maintaining the highest standards of hygiene in all production processes. Nevertheless the market has demanded an ever-increasing focus on not only hygiene and food safety standards since the 1980s, but also on microbiological testing and traceability of fresh food products. The Group built Westward Laboratories on a site in Callington adjacent to Ginster's Lynher Bakery in 1992 to handle the Group's testing requirements. Since its inception Westward has grown into one of the UK's leading independent food testing laboratories, well known for the quality of its work.

Westward has seen its workload increase dramatically in the last few years, with the impact of several food-related safety scandals, most notably 'horsegate'. No Samworth Brothers products were involved in the issue, but products from several other food manufacturers were found to contain horsemeat. It is clear the situation sharpened public attention on the content of their food. "The commercial world really wasn't ready for horsegate. There were tests available, but they were not being used sufficiently," says Westward General Manager Dr Nicola Wilson. "We don't do meat speciation testing in house – our testing facilities are focused on microbiological safety issues – but we coordinate that activity for the whole group. Testing has become both more intensive and more varied. Not only speciation, but

testing for allergens is much higher priority now, as is backing up the authenticity of marketing claims made on food packaging – how can you prove that a product is made with Sicilian lemons or Madagascan vanilla, for example?"

Westward, as a consequence of these pressures, has grown its team by about a third in the last ten years. It is clear to Nicola Wilson and the Westward team that food safety in today's world calls for shorter supply chains with more transparency as to where ingredients are actually being produced, a trend that fits well with the philosophy of local sourcing in Samworth Brothers.

RIGHT: *The Westward Laboratories team at work at their laboratory in Callington, Cornwall in 2015.*

large scale introduction of robotics. Nearly every product Ginsters bakes is now wrapped, boxed and palletised by robot. With a pastry product, rather than some of the more robust materials used on automated lines, this is a complex operation which requires high levels of precision and care. "Once the products have been baked and cooled, nothing we do to them adds any value. So that's why we introduced the robots," says Mark Duddridge. "But it is a complicated process. Not everything turns out the same shape, and handling products without damaging them is obviously very important."

Kensey Foods

Kensey Foods was spun off from Ginsters as an independent business in June 1997 and became Samworth Brothers' first dedicated desserts business. For some years, it was a successful business, for many years dedicated to Tesco. However by 2014 Kensey's performance was causing concern. High raw material prices plus changing market conditions started to have a huge impact on the business. At one point the Group was in negotiation with a potential buyer. However at the last minute it was decided to keep the business within the Group. Since then one area of increased focus at Kensey has been communication and staff engagement.

Jim Waller, now at Saladworks, but whose first role at Samworth Brothers was playing a part in the Kensey turnaround, says; "Since it was decided that the sale would not go ahead, the team at Kensey have lifted the place off the floor. What's the big change? It's all about communicating with people."

"We are still in a transition stage," says new Managing Director, Steve Hill. "We still have a lot of work to do. We had to go back to basics and reduce the complexity of the business. One really important event for us was when we took a bus of 25 staff up to Bradgate to look at their sites and get some interaction between the businesses. They all loved it. We had a talk in the bus on the way back and identified 72 points that Bradgate do and we wanted to start doing. We distilled that down to nine points — the Bradgate Nine — that each has someone in charge of and we wanted to focus on."

Cornish pasties were given European Union protection in 2011, meaning they can only be produced in Cornwall itself, after a long campaign in which Ginsters featured prominently. This gives the company a huge competitive advantage, but it also imposes pressures, especially to focus on the local origin of the product. Local sourcing has been a particular priority for Ginsters. It works closely with local meat and produce suppliers. One success has been to encourage local farmers to grow

ABOVE: *A Ginsters team setting off on the CHICKS (Country Holidays for Inner City Kids) Tri-Moor Cycle Challenge in 2014. The brand has been a keen supporter of the children's charity, based in Cornwall and Devon, for over 15 years.*

onions in Cornwall which means that up to 70 per cent of this vital ingredient is now sourced locally rather than from elsewhere in the UK.

But perhaps the biggest change in many years for Ginsters is the decision to spin off the route to market through which it became successful as a separate business. From 2015, Ginsters Van Sales Company will operate independently.

In the spirit of the new Samworth Brothers approach, which is far more focused on collaboration between businesses, Ginsters staff know the potential of the vans as a route to market, that for other Samworth Brothers companies, has not yet been explored. It is, essentially, a fleet that can get food up and down the country in any shape or form. For example, the company serves Costco stores with sandwiches on behalf of Melton Foods — that's nothing to do with Ginsters except its vans carry the stock.

The brand is also proud of its Cornish heritage and continues to play an active role in the community in Cornwall. It is a long term supporter of CHICKS (Country Holidays for Inner City Kids) and the Prince's Countryside Fund, a charity set up by HRH The Prince of Wales to support rural communities.

Across the road from the Ginsters bakery in Callington, Tamar Foods has been a separate business since 1999, focusing on baking pies, pasties, rolls and traditional hand crimped pasties under retailers' own labels. During that time, the site has seen a huge amount of change in terms of products and customers: on occasion it has served as a development site, initially with ready meals and Yorkshire puddings which ultimately transferred to Kettleby Foods and Charnwood, and desserts, which moved to Kensey Foods, plus also fried foods, which has subsequently moved to Brooksby Foods — all companies now within the Group.

Today the site has a number of specialisms, including premium hot pies, notably for Marks & Spencer and Tesco, multipack sausage rolls, especially very small snacking products, for Tesco, The Co-operative and Waitrose as well as its traditional Cornish pasty business, both machine and hand crimped. Tamar supplies nearly all the major retailers with hand crimped pasties, and actively supports Ginsters manufacturing hot pie and multipack rolls.

ABOVE: *The Ginsters brand message getting out on the road. Keith Suffling, from Samworth Brothers Supply Chain, Callington with an SBSC vehicle in the Ginsters livery.*

The business employs around 450 people, many of whom have over 25 years' service. It remains highly seasonal with a big and growing Christmas business and a busy hot pie season. The pace of change continues in the bakery as it adapts to its new customer base and their expectations with changes of organisation, operating procedures and investment in in-line pie manufacture, new washrooms, robotics and new snack roll packing technologies.

THIS PAGE: *Walkers Deli & Sausage Co Development Technician Joel Geyer in a new Innovation Centre that was opened at the Cobden Street site in 2014.*

THE WALKERS STORY

After the milestone of the new Charnwood Bakery, the Group's Walkers' businesses have grown and developed in an extraordinary way over the past three decades and given birth to a host of new enterprises.

After the building of the Charnwood Bakery, Walkers continued to go from strength to strength. By 1993 sales had reached £23 million and its profit, before interest, of £3 million was equal to the company's turnover when it was acquired and nearly twice the amount paid for its acquisition. Tesco and Waitrose had also developed to be key customers of Charnwood, and both are valued customers across the Group to this day.

Brian Stein's arrival at Charnwood as Managing Director in 1995 was the first of a number of key personnel changes that would have significant influence on the development of the Samworth Brothers Group. Lindsey Pownall, the current Group Chief Executive, who had previously been with Northern Foods at its Trafford Park Bakery, joined Charnwood as Commercial Manager in December 1995, and later took over from Brian as Managing Director. She was, she says, astonished at the level of customer care Walkers provided: "I'm a commercial person through and through, but I reckon I didn't know anything about dealing with customers until I joined Samworth Brothers. The lesson that was most valuable was from Peter Harris. He absolutely loved the customers. Well, I was used to production people who had a much more adversarial relationship, but that wasn't this guy's attitude — he'd do anything to keep the customer happy. In food manufacture, what you might be asking of the production director could amount to a whole lot of added complexity that's going to undermine his performance. But Peter, it didn't worry him. That drove huge customer confidence in the business. It was known in the trade that Walkers was the supplier you wanted to deal with."

Walker & Son still thrives today. The Group's foundation in pork butchery may have led on to activities such as ready meals and sandwiches, but Walker & Son is still the biggest pork pie manufacturer in the UK.

Charnwood Bakery recently celebrated its 25th anniversary and has benefited from an additional investment over recent years to further develop its bakery facilities. And the company has also gone back into the retail market, opening the first true Walkers shop in many years in Cheapside, Leicester.

Managing Director Peter Quinn, who joined the company in 2007

ABOVE: *Walker & Son master pie maker, Ian Heircock takes the Supreme Champion Award at the National Pie Awards in 2010.*

from Tamar Foods, says the 2008 economic downturn had a mixed impact for Walkers. "No business escaped the upheaval of the recession, but for us it was also a time of renaissance," he explains. "We have doubled our sales since 2007 turning over £80 million this year. 2014 was our record year. We represent the DNA of the business, going back quite a long time. We try to live by the Group's principles and embody the values." Walkers deals with every major UK retailer under either private label or its brands. It is the sole supplier of pies to Marks & Spencer and Waitrose. It has won many awards for its products — eight prestigious Q (for Quality) Awards in the last five years, and was among the first ten companies to get Marks & Spencer's coveted Plan A award for sustainability.

Pork pies might not seem a dynamic growth business, but Peter Quinn says that Walkers is increasing its growth opportunities. "We now export to eight countries with our Dickinson & Morris brand," he says. "What made that possible is that we developed a new process

that allowed the freezing of pies, and when you defrost them they're still crisp."

With the transfer of pie making to Charnwood, Cobden Street was adapted as a self-contained plant to supply Walkers' other products and continued to do well, supplying the Walkers shops as well as selling through retailers such as Waitrose and Tesco. In 1996 it was split off to form an independent company named Walkers Midshire Foods. The purpose of this was to create a separate identity for Walkers' sausage and cooked meats production, to simplify what had become a multi-site business, and to allow an increased management focus on what was then the smallest part of Walkers' turnover while eliminating distractions from the Charnwood management team.

At that time Midshire Foods produced a wide range of cooked meats, including traditionally cured hams, which were cured by an old and lengthy method, and up to 100 tons of sausage per week at peak times, as well as haslet, brawn, pork hocks, pork dripping and pork lard, which were made because they were among the traditional wares of pork butcher shops.

ABOVE: *HRH the Prince of Wales and the Duchess of Cornwall try their hand at making pork pies on a visit to the Ye Olde Pork Pie Shoppe in 2011. Also pictured are Brian Stein and Stephen Hallam.*

The creation of Midshire Foods represented another example of Samworth Brothers spotting a trend in consumer demand and achieving a great success as a result. Notwithstanding, the great liking for sausages among the British food-buying public, it must be admitted that the sausage had, at least until the early 1990s, received a bad press for many years. Poor quality sausages were all too common, and the sausage was regarded by many as a cheap, low quality food. The last 20 years, though, have in many ways seen the renaissance of the British

Championing food heritage

When a prospective customer asked the Walker & Son team to make a 'Melton Mowbray' pie that in no way resembled the real thing because 'it isn't against the law', the then Group Chief Executive Brian Stein had something of a light bulb moment.

He recalled, "I realised if they were right, traditional British food would cease to exist. Like the French or the Italians we should go for 'Geographic Indicator' status."

A Protected Geographical Indication (PGI) is one of three European designations created to protect regional foods that have a specific quality, reputation or other characteristics attributable to that area.

So Samworth Brothers backed the campaign led by the Melton Mowbray Pie Association to protect the unique 'Melton Mowbray' pie with PGI status and this landmark was achieved in 2009. The company has always been a strong champion of local sourcing and regional food heritage. Ginsters also campaigned for a similar

geographic indicator status to be given to the Cornish pasty, which was granted in 2011.

So what are the original features of a Melton Mowbray pork pie? The sides of a Melton Mowbray Pork Pie are bow-shaped as they are baked free standing, whereas most other pork pies are baked in hoops. The meat used is fresh pork which is naturally grey when cooked. The meat must be particulate, using chopped pork, rather than minced meat. The Melton Mowbray Pork Pie is also well jellied, the meat seasoned with salt and pepper, and it must be made in certain parts of Leicestershire and Nottinghamshire.

A genuine Cornish pasty has a distinctive 'D' shape and the pastry edges are crimped to one side of the pasty. The filling for the pasty is made up of uncooked minced or roughly cut chunks of beef (not less than 12.5%), swede, potato and onion with a light seasoning. No artificial flavourings or additives must be used. And, of course, it must be made in Cornwall.

sausage, and Samworth Brothers has played a key part. Sausages with natural casings, for example, are far superior to those with artifical ones, but they are harder to make and package.

Midshire Foods was the first manufacturer to find a way to automate the packaging of naturally cased sausages (using machines designed by its own staff) and its products represent the premium sausage range for most of its customers — and have achieved great success.

Midshire Foods' ham business also flourished after its split from Charnwood. In 1999, Tesco asked it to start supplying pre-packed, sliced ham for the first time, despite Midshire Foods having no slicing experience and the market being dominated by cheap hams manufactured not for their quality but for their efficiency on a slicing machine. Tesco had gone for quality — bucking the trend in the market for sliced cooked meats — and Midshire Foods did not let its customer down, successfully launching the highest quality sliced ham in the UK to good levels of sales.

Midshire Foods can also lay claim to playing a key role in the long-term development of the Samworth Group, because it was here that the next generation of the Samworth family took its first steps into executive

ABOVE: *Steve Walsh, former captain of Leicester City Football Club, Kelley North, Walkers shop Assistant Manager, Sarah Jennings, Walker & Son Purchasing Manager and Peter Quinn, Walker & Son Managing Director, open the new Walker & Son Cheapside shop in 2013.*

ABOVE (RIGHT): *Crowds on the opening day of the new Walker & Son shop in Cheapside in Leicester in 2013.*

management. Mark Samworth became Managing Director of Midshire Foods in 1996, shortly after the business split from Charnwood.

Midshire Foods remains a hugely important part of the Samworth Brothers Group. The Cobden Street operations have grown hugely, now turning over more than £100 million. But with growth comes added complexity, and Midshire Foods has been through some tough times of late.

Group Executive Director Anita Barker took over responsibility for the business in November 2013. "I joined originally to look after the cooked meats business. That had been hugely successful, based on supplying quality sliced ham. However by the time I arrived the business had also moved into moved into managing other sliced cooked meat categories which had become very challenging. We needed to think hard about how we organised the business for the future."

Anita Barker has split the Midshire Foods business into two, one covering sausage and the other cooked meats. These are now managed completely separately as two different companies, Walkers Deli and Walkers Sausage Co. Another development has been a stronger focus on category management and developing an understanding of the needs of the end consumer doing their shopping. A successful food manufacturer today not only has to have well invested facilities, but also has to invest in other ways, such as purchasing appropriate consumer data and research to inform its operations. As Anita Barker explains: "Increasingly data is like another piece of kit for us, and it can cost you between £100,000–£200,000. It's a piece of kit you can't see, and because you can't see it, in the past there was a reluctance to spend money on it. We analyse data to understand how shopping habits are changing. We can see exactly what people are spending on. We can see the impact of promotions, week by week."

The sausage business too has had its travails. The business, that could be said to have invented the premium sausage category, started to see

SAMWORTH PEOPLE

Simon Benning
Head of Development – Walkers Deli & Sausage Co

Simon started working for Samworth Brothers back in December 1997 as a development chef at Walkers Midshire Foods (as it was then called).

After some initial first day nerves, when he got lost on his way to the site in Leicester, he soon found his stride. He brought fresh ideas from his experience in restaurant and hotel kitchens into new product development, introducing new flavour combinations and the use of fresh herbs to create new ranges. Keeping up with changing consumer tastes and diet trends continues to be a challenging but vital part of his job.

Simon estimates he has helped to develop over 1,000 products while at Walkers Deli & Sausage Co.

Over the years, Simon has seen the size and scale of the business grow dramatically. From just 15 lines in 1997 to over 100 now, there has been significant site expansion, increased turnover, and diversification into new product areas, as well as new customers coming on board. Compared to just one when he first started, he and his team now work closely with five different retail product developers and buyers spanning premium pre-pack cooked meats, sausages, burgers and meatballs, hot deli snacking and deli.

For Simon, working at Samworth Brothers feels like belonging to one big family, and with that comes desire to deliver the traditions and values of the family. As part of that, Simon and his team, and everyone at Walkers Deli & Sausage Co, has a real pride and passion in everything they do.

competitors catch up. At one point, in 2014, Walkers was forced to make 150 people redundant. Anita Barker explained, "It was very painful, but we were able to reach a positive outcome by placing everyone who wanted this option into a job at another Samworth Brothers business. The number of businesses we have is a huge asset in that respect." The new Walkers Deli and Walkers Sausage Co now share a new innovation centre at Cobden Street in another example of increased collaboration across the Group.

Samworth Brothers' other connection back to its earliest roots is the old firm of Dickinson & Morris in Melton Mowbray — which markets itself as Ye Olde Pork Pie Shoppe. Founded by John Dickinson

ABOVE: *The Olympic torch passes Ye Olde Pork Pie Shoppe in 2012 on its way to the 2012 London Olympic Games.*

LEFT: *Dickinson & Morris Managing Director Stephen Hallam celebrated 160 years of business, in period costume.*

in 1851 and acquired by Samworth Brothers in 1992 after a fire had destroyed the interior, the shop was lovingly restored to create an olde worlde atmosphere.

The shop re-opened in November 1992 with a staff of 18 and Stephen Hallam as General Manager. Today the shop is an established Melton Mowbray attraction recognised by the East Midlands, English and British Tourist Boards, and a visit is part of Melton's tourist trail. Pie making demonstrations and tastings are regularly hosted in the shop for guests, who also learn about the long and distinguished history of the pork pie.

Dickinson & Morris was also a key player in the campaign to win Protected Geographical Origin from the EU for the Melton Mowbray pie. This means that only pies made in and around the town to the traditional recipe can carry the Melton Mowbray label.

The Melton Mowbray shop had a further refit in June 2014 and goes from strength to strength. Stephen Hallam is a regular 'pie expert' guest on national and regional TV and radio, espousing the qualities of the Melton Mowbray pork pie and Dickinson & Morris pies. The brand is also a keen supporter of the annual National Pie Awards, hosted in Melton Mowbray.

NEW DIRECTIONS

Adaptability is an important aspect of any successful business. The Ginsters and Walkers acquisitions were successful with subsequent periods of strong growth. However as consumer eating habits and lifestyles developed, a new generation of Samworth Brothers businesses also began to emerge.

ABOVE: *Kettleby Foods became the Group's first dedicated ready meals facility in 1999.*

LEFT: *An early picture of the Bradgate Bakery production team.*

During the 1980s Samworth Brothers had observed the fast-growing market for sandwiches that by 1991 was worth £1.8 billion a year. All the major supermarkets were selling sandwiches, as were Boots and hundreds of garage forecourts and small grocers throughout the UK. All these outlets were the very markets served by both Ginsters and Walkers, and it was seen that sandwich making would fit very well with the Group's activities — in making, marketing and distribution.

It was at a time when Samworth Brothers was thinking about sandwiches that it was approached by Tesco on the same subject. Sandwiches had become one of the fastest growing parts of Tesco's business and the company wished to secure adequate supplies for this growth market. Tesco asked Samworth Brothers to build a plant exclusively for sandwich production and committed to take a worth-while share of its output.

BELOW: *Early days at Bradgate. Angie Green, second left, shows how to make a perfect sandwich, as Polly Ahir, Shane Thorpe, Theresa Handley and Vicky Bines look on. November 1997.*

Despite all the inherent technical and servicing difficulties involved in the large scale production of sandwiches, Walkers was confident that it could develop the new skills required and bring fresh ideas into what had become a major industry. Tesco's needs provided the impetus for Walkers to go ahead and build a facility especially geared to sandwich making on the Beaumont Leys site at Leicester. The strategy was to establish Walkers in the sandwich business with one strong initial effort rather than to begin with nothing and build up. The new plant, named Bradgate Bakery, was to be equipped to operate a very large sandwich operation.

Bradgate Bakery was built on a six acre greenfield site at the cost of £6 million, of which £4 million was spent on machinery and equipment. Bradgate was built in a straight line to enable the bringing in of materials, and the manufacture, packing and dispatch of sandwiches to be a straightforward and logical procedure. In June 1993 the bak-ery started production of 11 varieties of sandwiches for Waitrose and Tesco; within 12 months it was becoming clear that the gamble of investing heavily to enter an unknown category was a good one.

With Bradgate's potential capacity of 50 million units a year, a study was put in hand to understand the requirements of the individual sandwich consumer and to forecast what Tesco's and Waitrose's initial requirements were likely to be. This was achieved by inviting senior people from Tesco and Waitrose to see the operation, to meet man-agement and staff members (and in particular the development chef) and to demonstrate the 'quality operation' that had been developed at Bradgate. The result of this exercise was that in July 1994 Tesco

BELOW: *David, Mark and John Samworth lay the foundation stone at Chetwode House, December 1997.*

transferred a substantial proportion of its £7 million sandwich business away from its other suppliers to Bradgate.

A successful campaign was then begun to set up a nationwide brand name for Ginsters sandwiches, a tactic which, if successful, would result in the first national independent sandwich brand. Just ten years previously the only chilled displays in small shops (such as newsagents) were a few tins of soft drinks, but by 1994 a small refrigerator offering a choice of sandwiches was a common sight in shops and forecourts.

In 1994 a trading partnership was made between Walkers Bradgate Bakery and Ginsters to market Bradgate-produced sandwiches nationwide. It marked a new era of collaboration between Group businesses and proved to be a highly successful venture. One aspect that contributed to the success was a radical restructure of the Ginsters van sales fleet to offer a seven day a week service to customers. Starting with a range of the ten known best-selling sandwiches, the strategy worked and, within a year, Ginsters' fleet of 85 vans had increased to 121, handling sandwiches in addition to its traditional products. To cope with their three-day life, sandwiches were manufactured, chilled, packed and delivered to customers with unprecedented speed. Orders arriving at Leicester by noon had been made on the same working day. Big retail customers were supplied direct from Leicester while Ginsters' vans supplied thousands of smaller customers all over the UK. To help deal with this large and complex operation, all van salesmen

ABOVE: *Melton Foods' purpose-built sandwich bakery in Melton Mowbray, set amongst landscaped gardens. A special walkway allows visitors to view the entire length of the production line.*

ABOVE (LEFT): *The newly completed Chetwode House, September 1998.*

were issued with hand-held computers which added up and printed invoices, and reconciled accounts.

Recruited from Northern Foods, Mark Duddridge became Managing Director of Bradgate in 1996, the same year the bakery won a coveted *Management Today* Best Factory award. Weekly production exceeding one million sandwiches in 1997 saw the plant exceed its original 50 million units per year capacity, and an extension, at a cost of £750,000, was necessary to keep up with production requirements. Further extensions to the bakery doubled the original footprint during 2000-2001 at a cost of £6 million. (There was a further extensive upgrade and extension of the Madeline Road site in 2010/11.) After the successful launch of Melton Foods as an independent business, of which more later, Mark left to become Managing Director of Ginsters in 1999, and was replaced by Lindsey Pownall. The company continued to grow further, reaching a turnover of almost £70 million in 2005.

The development of the Bradgate sandwich business proved that Samworth Brothers need not be in any way constrained by its historical areas of expertise. Pies, pasties, sausages and ham might be the products the company had always known since the Parr's days, but the Samworth Brothers mode of operations was, it had become abundantly clear, perfectly suited to being applied to other food lines. This was just as well, since the Group's key supermarket customers, led by Tesco, which at the time was in the early stages of the explosive growth that has led it to dominate the UK retail business, were repeatedly coming to Samworth Brothers in search of new products to satisfy their customers.

Also in the 1990s prepared meals started to become a big growth area of the food industry. Social changes, such as an increase in the number of households in which both partners work full-time, longer working hours for many, and a greater commitment to leisure time, meant that more people preferred not to cook when they got home in the evening. Samworth Brothers' first involvement with ready meals came about as a result of a trial operation set up at the Tamar Bakery in Cornwall to produce chilled recipe dishes on behalf of Tesco. The immediate success of this operation made it clear, though, that a dedicated facility would soon be needed. The sandwich operation too needed a new plant, as Waitrose, another key group customer, was looking to push more business Samworth Brothers' way, and the fierce competition between the supermarkets mean they prefer their rivals not to be supplied from the same bakery. At the same time, it was clear that the Group's corporate centre — even though it was and is, by design, extremely small — could not adequately be managed out of a suite of offices in the Charnwood plant. To this end, therefore, in 1997, the Group resolved to develop a substantial site on the edge of Melton Mowbray, with a new Group Centre, and space to build two manufacturing businesses.

BELOW: *Kettleby Foods was the Group's first dedicated meals business.*

Anita Pickering

Despatch and Stores Area Manager, Bradgate Bakery

Anita Pickering's first day at Cobden Street (a predecessor of Bradgate Bakery Madeline Road) was a memorable one; it was also the first day that the small site launched its sandwiches into Tesco!

As Bradgate Bakery's second longest serving employee, Anita was there at the start back in early January 1993. She joined a small sandwich making operation based at Cobden Street in Leicester, where she made sandwiches for Waitrose and Tesco around a table for the first few months, before the bakery moved to bigger premises at Madeline Road in June that year.

In those early days there were just 14 people making around 600 sandwiches a day, now Bradgate Bakery operates out of two sites with 1,500 staff.

Over her 22 years at Samworth Brothers, Anita has always worked for Bradgate Bakery, but her skills and experience have also been utilised to help set up other sites around the Group from Melton Foods and Saladworks to most recently, Bradgate Bakery Ashton Green.

Now as Despatch and Stores Area Manager, Bradgate Bakery Madeline Road and Ashton Green, she has a lot of responsibility on her shoulders but she still enjoys every day, not least as many of her colleagues are like family members to her.

Anita remembers fondly bakery visits from Sir David, and his real interest in the people working there. For her, working for a family business means that people always come first and that the family principles of People, Quality and Profit underpin everything that the Samworth Brothers Group does.

One of those was Melton Foods, which became a second sandwich manufacturing facility for the Group. The other was named Kettleby Foods, and became the Group's first dedicated ready meals plant. Kettleby moved into its £15 million, 60,000 square feet facility in April 1999.

Another area of development for the group in the late 1990s was desserts. Kensey Foods, Samworth Brothers' first dedicated desserts business, was spun off from Ginsters as an independent business in June 1997, producing a wide range of puddings for major supermarket clients, as well as a range of savoury pies. The firm became a dessert-only producer in 1998 — a long-time strategic goal that allowed the team to concentrate on one product range, lines such as custard

tarts, fruit tarts and steamed puddings. Later on, though, the firm moved into other dessert areas, notably chilled products such as cream scones, strawberry tarts and banoffee pie. Other Samworth Brothers dessert sites would follow, but more of that in a later chapter.

If all these expansions weren't enough, there was also a move into the chilled salads business with the April 2003 opening of Saladworks. The Group's involvement with pre-packaged salads began in 2001, when Bradgate Bakery began producing salads for Tesco, but with Bradgate at absolutely full capacity it was clear that a larger, dedicated facility would be needed if the business was to flourish. Today Saladworks has developed into a ready meals facility that works closely with Kettleby Foods. Brooksby Foods, originally an offshoot of Kettleby, has also been established. Again these further additions have their own stories to tell later on in this edition.

With these developments and other successes elsewhere in the Group, the scene was set for a period of sustained growth for the business through the late 1990s and beyond.

ABOVE: *Saladworks, completed in 2003, designed to be at the cutting edge of food safety, energy efficiency and environmental awareness, whilst offering exceptional staff facilities.*

Distribution, the Samworth way

Another Samworth Brothers business that came of age at this time was Samworth Brothers Distribution. (Renamed Samworth Brothers Supply Chain in 2015). Distribution is a crucial part of any business, and in the chilled food sector, where shelf life is key to success, it is absolutely central. Most — indeed virtually all — large companies nowadays contract out distribution to a specialist third party logistics provider, in accordance with the widely-accepted business philosophy that companies should focus on what they do best, and bring in outside parties for all non-core activities. The Samworth way, however, was a little different.

Walkers' distribution fleet, back in 1987, consisted of four vehicles. As the business grew, though, so did the requirement for transport, and, after short-lived experiments with third party hauliers that were not a complete success, it became clear that building a substantial distribution operation was the only way to guarantee customer service. There was also a belief that, with the right investment, Samworth Brothers Distribution could become a significant and successful business in its own right.

Woodside Distribution Depot was opened in December 1997, and was purpose-built on a six acre site close to the M1 at Leicester. This site was expected to be large enough to support the distribution needs of the entire Samworth Brothers Group for at least seven years but, by May 2000, the depot was at full capacity. An extension was built, providing refrigerated warehousing — almost doubling the existing

ABOVE: *Samworth Brothers Distribution Centre at Woodside Leicester.*

capacity — along with another 5,000 square feet of office accommodation. A further extension added another 30,000 square foot chilled chamber in 2007 as volumes continued to expand.

The business also had a number of vehicles based in Bristol and Cornwall. In 2006 SBD, as it was then, extended its Bristol operation when it moved into its current Patchway depot. Bristol is a key crossover point between the South West bakeries and the rest of the UK distribution network. Product coming up from the South West is cross docked there for onward distribution direct to retail depots or for onward trunking to Leicester for consolidation with Midlands bakery volume at Woodside.

Another smaller but important out-base was opened in Penrith which forms an ideally placed crossover point between the Midlands and Scotland for all Scottish depot deliveries.

THIS PAGE: *Blueberry Foods opened in 2008 as a desserts business.*

OPPOSITE: *David Samworth accepting the Business of the Decade award from the Rt Hon Patricia Hewitt at the Leicestershire Business Awards 2003. Also pictured are Brian Stein and Nick Townsend of Wilson Bowden.*

GROWTH
AND CHANGE

From a business turning over £1 million a year in 1978, just after Ginsters was purchased, the company had been transformed by 2005 to a Group with more than 5,500 staff and an annual turnover of £450 million. More strong growth followed. However by 2010 it was clear the business needed to respond to shifting market conditions.

By 2005 strong growth levels were being achieved in both the long established Samworth Brothers businesses and the newer ventures such as Bradgate Bakery and Kettleby Foods. Seen from the perspective of the Ginsters business that the Samworth brothers bought in 1977, with a turnover of only £1 million, the growth of the company was little short of miraculous.

In 2003 David Samworth and Brian Stein accepted the 'Business of the Decade' award at the Leicestershire Business Awards, just one of a host of awards won by the company around this time. In 2005 Ginsters became the second Samworth business, after Bradgate, to win a *Management Today* Best Factory award. In the same year Ginsters was also named UK Food Company of the Year by *Management Today,* perhaps the supreme honour in the food manufacturing industry.

2005 was a significant year with the retirement of David Samworth as Chairman of the Group, to be replaced by Nick Linney, previously a Samworth Brothers Non-Executive Director for close to a decade.

BELOW: *Coldcall is a successful part of Samworth Brothers 'small wheels' logistics offer. As with most new Group businesses, Coldcall was launched — in 2008 — as an entrepreneurial and innovative response to a customer need.*

Bob Oxley
Ginsters Van Sales Driver

Bob Oxley started as a Van Salesman just over 36 years ago in 1979. He saw the job advert in his local paper and was lucky to get the job out of 130 applicants. Many of the drivers he met on his first day are still friends today.

Back then, his route covered the Swindon and Gloucester areas when the only customers served were fish and chip shops, butchers, bakers and pubs. Proving how much the business has changed over the years, Ginsters Van Sales now serve a different range of customers including petrol forecourts, convenience stores and supermarkets. Back then it was nearly all cash business on manual invoices so Bob had to know the price of each product to complete the invoice.

After a couple of years on the road, he was promoted to Supervisor to assist with the increase in vans and sales. He moved to regional relief and covered journeys in all sales offices, with the exception of Cumbria and Milton Keynes which were the latest ones to open.

While on regional relief duty, he enjoyed meeting people from all across the UK, and while he met some great people along the way, he found the Scottish people especially friendly!

Now at the age of 66, Bob is still enjoying his job covering Somerset and Wiltshire and says

that he really can't imagine himself not doing his job any more as it is such a big part of his life.

He is proud to have been part of the Samworth Brothers' success over the years, and feels that his input into this success has been appreciated by everyone he works with.

With Brian Stein continuing as Group Chief Executive the years from 2005 to 2010 were a period of continued strong growth for the company. Annual group turnover rose from £462 million in 2005 to £716 million in 2010 during this period.

Other businesses emerged during this period. In 2008 Blueberry Foods was opened. Located in Leicester Forest East, adjacent to the M1, and next door to Saladworks, it was built originally to supply cheesecakes and other chilled desserts to Marks & Spencer. Also in the same year Coldcall was launched. Each new Samworth Brothers business has usually sprung from the entrepreneurial spirit of Samworth Brothers people. Coldcall is a good example of this. Dave Lewis, who set up Coldcall and still works in the business, remembers its initial

Paula Gagin
High Care Production Manager, Melton Foods

'If at first you don't succeed, try again', was Paula's mantra after an unsuccessful first interview at Bradgate Bakery. She reapplied a few years later and started as a Production Operative on the PM shift there in 1995 where she made Ginsters sandwiches.

That first day, 19 years ago, feels like yesterday says Paula. Having come from the meat industry, she recalls being struck by the impressive site facilities, focus on quality and the smell of fresh ingredients.

After taking on a variety of production and managerial roles in the bakery, she was asked to join the project team to set up Saladworks, a new site in Leicester back in 2003.

This was an exciting and challenging time, helping with recruitment, machine trials, and customer presentations. She remembers a visit from Sir David Samworth to Saladworks just before she was about to embark on a year's sabbatical in Australia, and his insistence that she returned to Samworth Brothers afterwards.

A week after arriving back in the UK she started at Melton Foods where she is now a High Care Production Manager. This role brings her much job satisfaction, especially motivating her team and sharing their achievements, as people make Samworth Brothers what is it today, according to Paula.

Over her years at Samworth Brothers, she has seen the business grow and keep pace with changing industry and economic climates by constantly adapting, improving and innovating.

Being a family business has also given Samworth Brothers a point of difference, instilling a sense of consistency and stability from generation to generation, which is felt by everyone who works for the Group.

birth. "I had just left Northern Foods and I got a call from Brian Stein saying there was an idea in the business to set up logistics business that would deliver Day 1 product into Tesco on the same day. I remember Lindsey Pownall coming round to see me at home and we talked about the idea round my kitchen table," said Dave Lewis.

The business initially focused on servicing Tesco stores in central London but proved to be so successful there was a national roll out. The business currently has a fleet of 40 vans and depots in Falkirk, Durham, Warrington, Leicester (Ashton Green), Milton Keynes and Bristol. The Tesco connection continues with Coldcall delivering in product to Tesco petrol forecourts and Tesco coffee shops. However its client base has also developed to include, via Melton Foods, John Lewis coffee shops and Costco.

In 2009 Tamar Foods also took over the small Duchy Originals' Cornish bakery and the business was renamed Duchy Desserts.

At existing businesses there was major investment with the installation of leading edge robotics technology at Ginsters in 2006 and at Kensey with the K2 extension in 2007. In 2008 Kettleby Foods also opened a satellite site close by at Pate Road in Melton Mowbray.

However for Samworth Brothers, as for pretty much every other business, the world changed in 2008 when the global economy collapsed. Twenty years of continuous growth had left the Group with an understandable sense of impregnability and, initially at least, the recession had at most a marginal effect on the Group's business. The Group's sales actually rose by five per cent in that year and its strong balance sheet, with no debt to service, meant that it was comfortably able to stick to its investment plans.

It was at the end of 2010 that the recession truly hit Samworth Brothers. Why there was this two year delay can only be guessed at: perhaps the Group's top of the marketplace position gave it some protection. "2010 was a record year," says Mark Samworth. "But after that, when sales started to become much harder to win, it became clear that we probably weren't challenging ourselves enough."

One possible influence is that eating out is one of the first things people cut back on when times are tough. So it's not totally surprising that a group focused on products for eating at home should continue to do reasonably well in the early stages of a recession.

"For whatever reason, we maintained strong performances longer than anyone else in the industry, but paradoxically that probably hurt us," says Lindsey Pownall. "Our competitors had felt the heat sooner, and thus they were two years ahead of us in adapting to the new world."

Samworth Brothers hit a perfect storm in 2010; not only did sales growth slow, but commodity prices rose dramatically too. Additionally, the Group's retailer customers were floundering, trying to adapt to a different world after years of nonstop growth. "It was an article of faith at Samworth Brothers that the key to success was listening to customers,"

says consultant Alex Knight, who has worked with the Group for 25 years. "But the customers were saying 'Help us! Be proactive. Come up with new ideas. We are just a distribution channel for you.'"

Commodity prices generally — whether pork or oil, notwithstanding the drop in the oil price during 2014 — have been on an upward trend for many years, and this added to the problems the various Samworth Brothers companies faced around 2010. There were many reasons that commodities have gone up, but certainly the strength of markets like China played a part. Obviously a farmer in England is unlikely to be thinking about selling his pigs to China, but that market has swept up a lot of European pork in recent years, and the result is there is less supply to existing markets.

"For a bunch of reasons, our margins have come under extreme pressure. The response to tough times has to be to find new markets where we can make the margins we need to make the investments we want," says Mark Samworth.

ABOVE: *Group Holdings Board — 2011. Left to right, Les Atkinson, Jonathan Warburton, Lindsey Pownall, Mark Samworth, Nick Linney and Brian Stein.*

The situation led the Group and the individual businesses to interrogate the way they were operating. Over the previous years the emphasis had been keeping up with customer growth. There had been less focus on cost management or putting very sophisticated systems and processes in place to track the real profit drivers. This changed quickly.

The result of all this is that, for the first time in many years, several Samworth Brothers companies had to retrench. The Duchy Desserts site was closed in early 2015 and the business transferred into Kensey Foods. "I stood up in front of all the people in Duchy and told them I was extremely sorry that we were having to close the site — and I was," says Lindsey Pownall. "You have to genuinely have understanding and empathy if you're going to do it in a Samworth Brothers way."

Mark Samworth says he is proud of how the Group dealt with these reverses. "It sounds odd but I was hugely impressed by the way we handled the redundancies we have had to make in recent years," he says. "There is a right way to do it and a wrong way. I believe we've proved that we can deal with bad news in a way that is true to our culture and our values, and I am really pleased we did."

An increased focus on cost management has been at the heart of the Group's response to the changing market place. As a supplier generally focused on the top end of the market, it is built into the DNA of Samworth Brothers companies that the best response to a desire to reduce price is to increase quality, but all businesses have to focus on efficiency and drive out unnecessary cost. "For us to be a long-term

In November 2011 the Group was hit by tragic news when two Samworth Brothers Distribution drivers — Kye Thomas, who was based in Callington, and Terry Brice, who worked out of the SBD Bristol depot — were among seven people killed in a terrible accident on the M5 motorway. Another Samworth Brothers Distribution driver, John Clark, was also injured in the incident. The whole business was shocked and stunned by the news. At the Group site in Callington, Cornwall, there is now a garden of remembrance dedicated to the drivers, and there is a memorial plaque at the Samworth Brothers Distribution Bristol depot.

LEFT: *The Group played a part in the Queen's Diamond Jubilee celebrations in 2012 by creating the hampers supplied by Waitrose to the Jubilee concert at Buckingham Palace. A number of the Group businesses were involved and the hampers were packed at Melton Foods in an overnight high security operation.*

RIGHT: *Key members of the Jubilee hampers team in 2012 — front left, Mark Shippey, Group Technical Director; front right, Wendy Smith, Melton Foods Managing Director (now Managing Director of Kettleby Foods); back left, Paul Old, Bradgate Bakery Production Director; back right, Greg Rodenhurst, Melton Foods; with colleagues from Waitrose in the centre row, left to right, Jo Hensman, Paul Hogan and Tanya Mugford.*

The business had undertaken a similarly successful hamper operation for the Queen's Golden Jubilee in 2002, which led to the Group being asked to participate again in 2012.

business, we have to do things properly. We can't cut corners, but equally we cannot waste money. That's a tough balance to find," says Mark Samworth.

Retired Group Finance Director Alan Barton puts it best. "You can't just turn everything upside down," he says. "Our core strength is always going to be quality and innovation, but you do have to do a little bit of guerrilla warfare as well. You have to know much more about how your customers — and their competitors — are faring. What are we looking for in terms of development and what price point are we going to be able to sell it at? When you're chasing sales growth, being cost conscious is secondary. Even if you spend a little too much getting there, the momentum of growth means you catch up. But the central message on cost is: if it doesn't add value, you don't do it. We had to become very good at that very quickly."

THIS PAGE: *Brian Stein and Lindsey Pownall, outgoing Group Chief Executive and incoming Group Chief Executive, at Brian's retirement event at Kilworth Hall in April 2012.*

OPPOSITE: *Sir David Samworth talking to staff at a Chetwode House event in 2014.*

THE NEXT ERA

2012 saw the appointment of a new Group Chief Executive, Lindsey Pownall. The period 2012 to 2015 saw other new senior appointments and an increased focus on collaboration across the business.

Brian Stein joined Samworth Brothers in 1995 from Northern Foods and took over as Group Chief Executive in 1999. Under his direction, the group enjoyed a quite remarkable run of success, going from a £200 million business to one that turned over more than £800 million in little more than five years.

"Brian is the only CEO I know who can put his name behind an entirely straight line of growth," says Alex Knight. "It is a quite remarkable record. And he was brilliant. You would be having a conversation with him, and he'd say to you 'Next year, these three companies will go bust'. He was always right!"

Brian Stein announced his intent to retire in 2009. He left the company in 2012, at the age of 62, and was replaced by Lindsey Pownall, a long-time Group Executive Board Member, who had for several years held responsibility for several of the Group's businesses. Brian Stein currently serves as the Chairman of the Nottingham University Samworth Academies Trust.

"I found I had inherited an organisation that I didn't know a great deal about, aside from the businesses I had already been running," says Lindsey Pownall. "I had spent very little time with the Cornish operations, so I made sure to go down there a lot in my first few months. Every month I took all the directors in Cornwall out for dinner so they got to know me in a social environment."

Alongside Lindsey Pownall, Mark Samworth has seen his role within the group change dramatically in the last ten years. "Lindsey and Mark had to create a new relationship," says Alex Knight. "Everyone

now sees Mark and not David, and the Lindsey transition was a massive part of that. Mark has ensured that the family culture has endured. When the going gets tough and horrible decisions have to be made, family values win out."

Part of that change of role for Mark Samworth came about at the start of 2015, when he announced his intention to stand down from the Group Executive Board (GEB), of which he had been a member since its foundation. Mark continues as a member of the Group Holdings Board.

Jonathan Warburton, himself chair of a very large family owned food producer, has sat as a Non-Executive Director on the Samworth Brothers Holdings board for many years. "I have been a great advocate of Mark carving a new role for himself as an ambassador of the business," he says. "What Mark is realising is that he's the only person who can do that — because it's his name that's over the door. That will reinforce the family ethos."

"The job I need to do is the job that only I can do — because it is my family business," says Mark Samworth. "I have to be the unifying force for the Group, to get round the different businesses and protect our culture and values. That's what my father did for many years, and now it's what I must do."

The structure that David Samworth and Alex Knight created envisaged a group of independently managed companies that controlled their own destiny, each with its own board of four directors, plus a chairman from the corporate centre. The directors would manage the business as they saw fit, they would interact with suppliers

John Samworth

John Samworth retired from the Group Holdings Board in 1999 but continued to take a very keen interest in the business until his death in August 2014, aged 81. At the time of John's death, Sir David Samworth wrote this tribute for the *Samworth Standard*, the Samworth Brothers group staff newspaper.

"John was my brother but also my best friend. We were in business together for nearly 60 years. We both started work at the bottom of the company, when we left the army. It was a much smaller company then, just 30 or 40

people. John could do everything, make sausages, pork pies, black puddings and the rest. There was nothing in the business he could not do.

He was ahead of the time. At one point we had 34 shops and he was a great retailer. At that time it wasn't usual for shops to have refrigerated counters, but he insisted on them. He could see it was the future.

He was obsessed with product quality. When we drove from Leicester to Cornwall it would take at least six hours with John rather than the usual four. He would have us stop off in Evesham to visit a farm that grew, he said, the best plums in England and then in Somerset he would always visit a dairy that made excellent cheddar cheese. It was always about the product with John.

John wasn't just all about work. He had a very rounded life. He was very keen on his cricket and hockey and was a very good photographer. He was mad about cars and very knowledgeable about them.

He took a keen interest in the business right until the end. He was extremely bright but also had the most retentive memory, which is a powerful combination. We used to meet up most Fridays in the office to talk about the business, current trading conditions and the old times. He would always get the weekly figures every Tuesday night. He was a very special person and will be greatly missed by his family and his many friends."

LEFT: *John Samworth, 1932-2014*

and customers themselves, and they would be judged on their performance. Those businesses would be relatively small — they were ideally to max out at a turnover of about £25 million and about 200 employees. If they got bigger, the Group would look at ways to split them and spin off a new business.

That model served the Group well for 20 years, although the fact that Bradgate has reached a turnover of around £200 million and has 1,500 people working for it shows there has been some flexibility over time. But like every business, Samworth Brothers today is dependent for its continued success on its ability to manage a constantly changing environment, and the post-recession world it now finds itself in requires tweaks to the model.

"It's ingrained in our DNA — from Sir David ultimately — that we do things differently," says Gary Lewis, Group Director of Finance at Samworth Brothers. "We should never assume something that everyone else does is the right solution, but always analyse the situation from first principles."

Almost immediately after Lindsey Pownall became Group Chief Executive, Samworth Brothers embarked on the most extensive management development programme in its history. "There were three streams of more than 20 people going through the programme over an 18 month period — the top 65 directors from across the business," explains Alex Knight, who created and ran it. "It was a very challenging programme, partly because of the scale and partly because of the timing — the business was in a very tough place and dealing with bad numbers virtually every week. When things were really tough, many Chief Executives would have cancelled it, but Lindsey was absolutely committed."

That programme had a number of side effects. One, perhaps less planned than others, was to create much better networks between the directors of the individual companies, something that had not existed to any great degree beforehand. Directors were not encouraged to talk to their peers elsewhere in the Group, but to focus exclusively on their own company's performance. There was, to a certain extent, a sense of competition between the different operations, even to the extent of competing against each other for business. "It was almost 'Speak to your competitors before you talk to other Group companies'," says Alex Knight. "But the retailers were asking for more coherent and structured responses from suppliers, and so that had to change. There were examples of a number of the businesses going into the same meeting with the customer but with a limited amount of coordination and it inevitably comes across as less joined up than it can be," says Gary Lewis. "Now, we want one or two people going in, and we want to present a unified Samworth Brothers experience."

"Collaboration went from being a nice-to-have to a necessity," says Alex Knight. "Lindsey saw that, and realised it would be one of the biggest culture changes in the history of Samworth Brothers. All the research we have done is showing that the retailers want deeper, more intimate relationships."

LEFT: *Samworth Brothers wins the Family Business of the Year Award at the 2011 Private Business Awards. Left to right are Mark Samworth and Caroline Samworth, Grant Gordon, Director General of the Institute of Family Business; Charlie Hoffman, Managing Director, HSBC Private Bank (UK) Ltd; Ruby Parmar, Partner and Head of Private Business at PwC; and Ronni Ancona (awards presenter).*

Around the Group, the question of collaboration — and its cousin, category management — comes up in virtually every conversation. "Samworth Brothers is the best I have ever seen at managing relationships with its customers," says Jonathan Warburton. "That is why it grew — because it was very safe to go to. So the buyers think to themselves 'I don't need to worry about that, because Samworth is doing it'. Which is, as a supplier, the perfect place to be. But at the same time, providing solutions for retailers also has to be a core skill for the business. It is hard in private label, but that is a convenient excuse. You say 'If we were a branded supplier, what would we have to do?' — and you apply a bit of branded thinking to your business."

Although this change is taking place across the entire group, in truth it is a change that has to take place in the minds and psyches of individual managers. "We have got a lot better at sharing good practice across the Group," says Group Technical Director, Mark Shippey. "And it has gathered pace — accelerating that process has been one of

Lindsey's core objectives. But it is not about changing the structures of the organisation — it's about changing behaviours."

"Fifteen years ago, this was a pretty small business, and it's important to remember how far the Group has come in that time," says Ian Fletcher, a Director on the Group Executive Board. "It's been fortunate to have some really good relationships with the retailers and to grow with them. In the future I think we will have a lot more synergies as to how the businesses are run. There will be standard ways of working and standard key performance indicators. Decisions will be made more around data than gut feel."

Ian Fletcher had previous experience of Samworth Brothers in his long career at Tesco, before joining the Group in 2014.

"When I was a customer of Samworth Brothers," he says, "one always felt there was a passion and enthusiasm in the business for its customers and a big commitment to quality. It was a business that always did the right thing. Looking forward the retail landscape is changing fast. The challenge for the business will be to stay nimble and flexible, and ahead of the curve. We have to look over the horizon, see what's next and how we can respond in the best way."

This change in the Group's culture is coming from Lindsey Pownall; on that all executives across the Group are agreed. "I have focused on interdependence, which was largely ignored, in the past," she says. "We do all the federal things — letting executive teams run their own businesses — but we say to them 'You're wasting your time if you're not doing this for the greater good of the Group. You can't declare independence and do everything yourself. The customers won't let you'. But I definitely do not see us moving to a model with a great big central management setup. I have been here for 20 years and we used to speak of the units as independent businesses. I was Charnwood, I was Bradgate, I was Melton. That's who you were really working for. The family had not wanted a corporate identity, but I felt we needed an umbrella for the organisation. When I took over as Group Chief Executive, I was determined that everyone would say they worked for Samworth Brothers. The subsidiary is really important — it's your home, where you put your slippers on — but you work for Samworth Brothers. Now, when we go to customers, we sign in as Samworth Brothers. If we don't

LEFT: *Developing strong and enduring relationships with suppliers has always been an important value for the Group. Pictured here is Graham Stark, Managing Director of M&F Produce receiving the 2013 Supplier of the Year award from Lindsey Pownall and Jimmy Mark, now Managing Director of Blueberry Foods and (in 2013) responsible for group purchasing relationships. M&F Produce and Samworth Brothers have built a long-term partnership which has helped M&F Produce grow over the past decade from a business with fewer than 10 employees to one with more than 100 staff.*

ABOVE: *Mark Samworth with Group Holdings Board Director William Kendall.*

RIGHT: *Mark Samworth presents Les Atkinson with an appropriate retirement gift at the Directors' conference in 2013.*

do that, we dilute our influence with the customer. They want to see us that way. They like the name — people recognise it and they know what it stands for. So let's use it!"

In the period 2012 to 2015 there have been other changes and new appointments at Holdings Board and Group Executive Board level. Long-standing Holdings board director Les Atkinson, who had previously held senior positions in BP, stepped down in 2013. He had been a director since 1999 and made a significant contribution during this 14 year period.

Sadly, less than two years after this retirement, Les died after a short illness in early 2015. "His passing was a terrible shock," said Mark Samworth. "He received the British Empire Medal in the New Year's Honours List for his dedication to his local community, and it meant the world to him." Les had originally been recruited to add big company experience as well as financial acumen to the Samworth Brothers board. His contribution was much broader than that, though. According to Mark Samworth: "It was Les's personality that really made his role

work. His deep knowledge and insight was delivered with a great humility and, often, a dry wit that encouraged us to really think about what he said. I know he admired the ethos of our business and he shared our passion to build on it. That's why he was so effective."

A new director arrived on the Holdings Board in 2013. William Kendall is well known for his pioneering work with brands such as The New Covent Garden Soup Company and Green & Black's. During the same period there have also been new recruits. In 2013 Stephen Draisey joined the Group Executive Board and Anita Barker followed in 2014. Both had distinguished previous careers in food manufacturing. In 2014 Ian Fletcher also joined the Group Executive Board from Tesco plc. Also in 2014, following the retirement of Group Finance Director, Alan Barton, Richard Armitage joined as the new Group Finance Director. In 2015 two existing Managing Directors, Paul Davey, Managing Director of Bradgate Bakery and Mary-Ann Kilby, Managing Director of Melton Foods, also joined the Group Executive Board.

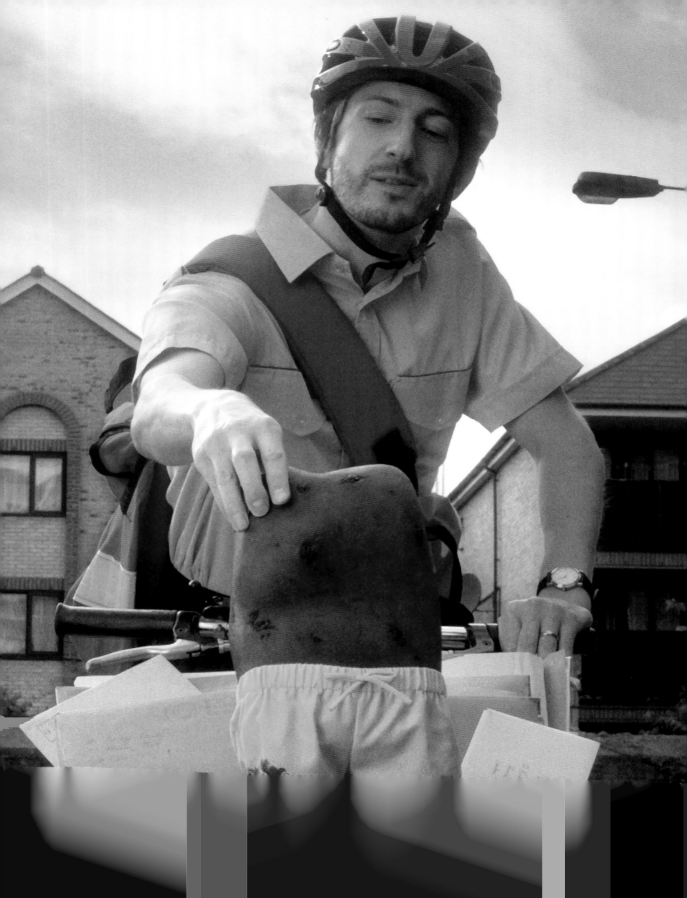

LOOKING TO
THE FUTURE

It is now more than 100 years since George Samworth laid the foundations of the business. Samworth Brothers is proud of its long history and heritage. However, as its sales approach £1 billion per annum, the business also has its eyes firmly on the future.

LEFT: *Just a few months after purchasing Soreen, the Group invested £3 million in a new TV advertising campaign for the brand featuring a new 'The Loveable Loaf' character.*

RIGHT: *The Bradgate Bakery Ashton Green site. A new £17 million investment by the Group in 2014.*

As we have seen, for many years, growth by acquisition was an important part of the growth of the Samworth business. From Frank Samworth's purchase of TN Parr right back in 1950 through to Pork Farms, Ginsters and Walkers, the family rarely shied away from investing in complementary businesses and bolting them on to their existing interests.

Somewhere along the line, Samworth's acquisitive nature changed. With the move into supplying the major supermarkets in the 1990s, and particularly the explosive growth of the sandwich and ready meals markets — and most importantly of all, the huge success of the Group's Tesco relationship, organic growth became more immediately appealing. Through the 1990s and the early part of this century, the Group followed this path on many occasions, giving birth to Tamar and Kensey Foods in Cornwall, plus Melton Foods, Kettleby Foods, Saladworks, Blueberry and Brooksby in Leicestershire.

BELOW: *Innovation on show at Bradgate Bakery for a VIP customer visit.*

ABOVE: *Bradgate Bakery Production Director Paul Old and Bradgate staff celebrate the first sandwich off the line at the new Ashton Green facility, just six months after ground was broken on the site.*

Growth has always been a central strategic goal for Samworth Brothers. For a time, though, that growth came relatively easily; living through the greatest boom in British retailing history as a key supplier of the main engine of that growth helped the Group to success. However, post the economic implosion of 2008, the situation changed dramatically. The overall UK retail market was at best flat and a number of UK retailers began to experience the sort of pains from which they had for many years seemed immune.

"We know organic growth is going to be harder to come by in the future, so growth by acquisition is going to be increasingly important for us," says Lindsey Pownall. "But we had not been involved in mergers and acquisitions work for so long, the process was always going to be tough."

Lindsey Pownall got to know, and formed a working relationship, with Tom Lindsay of London-based boutique M&A practitioner Spayne Lindsay. Founded in 2004, Spayne Lindsay specialises in the

food and beverage sector and has advised on a large number of UK-based deals — ideal partners for a group taking its first steps back into the acquisition market.

"We had known the company for years but hadn't had much to do with it," said Tom Lindsay. "They weren't that interested in talking to people like us, so we really only had the occasional contact at industry dinners. Then we were hired to sell Uniq, the major part of which was the sandwich business in Northampton. Samworth Brothers was a potential bidder, but eventually the business was sold to someone else, back in 2012. After that, I had a call from Lindsey to say 'I am taking over and we want to make acquisitions. Uniq was not successful for us, can you give us advice on our future approach and to think about what we might be able to do?" So Spayne Lindsay were more formally engaged to help create an acquisition strategy.

tl

LEFT: *Official opening of Bradgate Bakery Ashton Green in November 2014 including, directly in front of sculpture, left to right, Tesco Director of Convenience, George Wright; Lindsey Pownall; Leicester City Mayor, Sir Peter Soulsby; Tesco Chairman Sir Richard Broadbent and Mark Samworth.*

Lindsey Pownall describes the strategy she and Spayne Lindsay created. "We want to look at businesses that have a strong management team in place. We are not keen to look at turnaround situations because that would almost certainly mean more chilled foods, and why would we want more chilled foods? We wouldn't have the right experience to undertake turnaround situations in other sectors. So I would want a strong management team in there, possibly one that has been limited in terms of capital because of its ownership, and that might have also been starved of creativity for the same reason."

Another part of the strategy was dictated by the board. Group Finance Director Richard Armitage says: "One of the principles we work to is that we will not bet the farm. There is a desire to remain in the UK, to remain fairly close to food — so going right out of food and drink would not happen. But food does not need to be the staple things on your table."

Within such criteria deals don't happen overnight. "You can't force deals to happen," Tom Lindsay emphasises. "Samworth Brothers' biggest advantage is that they have cash and a great reputation in the market. They treat their businesses with a great deal of respect. If you're a seller of a business, and you're concerned about its future, they are a good potential purchaser." And that is how Samworth and Soreen came together.

Founded in the 1920s by Danish immigrant John Sorensen, Soreen is one of Britain's iconic food brands. So many of us ate the company's malt loaf product as children that its brand equity, even among those who have not eaten it for many years, remains strong.

Ironically, for many years, Soreen was owned by the Warburton group, whose chairman Jonathan Warburton is a long-time Samworth Brothers Non-Executive Director. Warburtons sold the company in 2003 to Interlink Foods, which was the start of a difficult decade for the malt loaf brand.

Interlink, unfortunately, went into administration in 2007 with large debts. Barclays was Interlink's lender, and it embarked on a period of assessment to see whether the assets could trade their way out of debt. Soon it was clear they couldn't, so the bank swapped debt for equity and became a 40 per cent shareholder in the business.

THE LOVEABLE LOAF

McCambridge Foods, a second generation family business, then bought Interlink out of administration. Barclays decided to take a bigger stake and in 2013 it was agreed the business was in a suitable place to be sold.

Paul Tripp, who had been with the Soreen business since 2007 as Technical Director and then Managing Director, takes up the story. "Samworth Brothers came to the front quite quickly," he says. "We had something of a meeting of minds — our approach to the balanced scorecard was very similar to their ideas about people, quality and profit — and the fact that this was an established, trusted brand was appealing to them. We went into exclusive talks with them. The deal went through in February 2014."

For Samworth Brothers, Soreen represented a slight change of direction. Its product is ambient, not chilled, and it owns its own brand, rather than being a private label operation like most of the Samworth

Brothers companies. But for Lindsey Pownall, the deal's significance is not particularly linked to these aspects. "What's most important about the Soreen acquisition is that it was safe for both the Group and the family, and it caused people to pay more attention," she says. "It being a branded business or an ambient business is secondary to this point. But it is a strong business, well managed and I think the brand can move into new areas. There is a great cultural fit — that was hugely important to us — and I think it will provide a great addition for us."

The acquisition of Soreen was one milestone in 2014, another, the opening of the Bradgate Bakery Ashton Green facility also highlighted that organic growth was still very much on the agenda. Paul Davey joined Bradgate Bakery as its new Managing Director in 2007, shortly before the financial crisis.

"Halfway through 2008, sandwich sales took a backward step. You'd have been better off being in tupperware boxes, loaves of bread or blocks of cheese," says Paul Davey. "There was a reaction from consumers, but it lasted only so long — the power of convenience takes control and things bounced back." Supermarket shoppers also started to have more money in their wallet because of lower interest rates.

Since then the business has moved forward significantly. Historically Bradgate Bakery and one other supplier each produced about half of Tesco's sandwiches. However in 2014, due to an issue with another supplier, the customer urgently required further additional capacity. Thus came about Samworth Brothers' first new build facility since the creation of Blueberry Foods in 2008. Bradgate's new Ashton Green bakery was built on a plot of land close to the original Madeline Road site, which the company had acquired some years previously in case of just such a need.

Unlike other businesses that may have needed to go to investors or financial institutions to secure funding to build a £15 million facility,

BELOW: Left to right, Melton Foods Sales Director Michelle Sanders, Paula Gagin, also Melton Foods, and Costa colleagues Hannah Mckay, Judith Jerodiaconou and Daksha Chohan on Costa launch day at Melton Foods.

Samworth Brothers had the capability to respond very quickly to meet the customer's needs. The facility was built in close partnership with Tesco. The plans were confirmed in late February 2014, and contractors broke ground on March 10. Remarkably just six months later the first trial sandwich went down the line on September 10th and by October the bakery was fully operational, with 350 people recruited and the facilities approved by Tesco. It was officially opened by the Tesco chairman Sir Richard Broadbent in November 2014.

The addition of Ashton Green has taken Bradgate, whose turnover, at around £200 million, is the largest of any Samworth Brothers business, to 1,500 employees. Davey says that the size imposes huge challenges on the company's management, if they are to live up to Samworth Brothers' standards of employee engagement.

One of the key challenges is to translate the feel of the business that has clearly made it successful, into a much larger environment. Paul Davey

ABOVE: *Dave Lewis, Chief Executive of Tesco, on a visit to Bradgate Bakery in April 2015. Pictured left to right, Matt Simister, Fresh Food and Commodities Commercial Director, Tesco; Clare Keers, Sales Director, Bradgate Bakery; Ian Fletcher, Samworth Brothers Group Executive Director; Dave Lewis; Jason Tarry, Chief Product Officer, Tesco; Lindsey Pownall and Tim Smith, Group Quality Director, Tesco.*

says: "In a smaller business, you can get your arms around it and have a personal relationship with all your staff. To do the same thing in a larger firm requires a lot more of the same from more people. We make sure we are in the bakery, talking to people, being visible; we have the same quarterly briefing process — it just takes longer because we have to do more of it. The directors and managers still serve Christmas dinner to all staff — I was tired by the end of eight days of it, especially since we'd been in three days until 3am serving the night shift. But for me it is hugely important not to lose that feel, just because we are bigger."

As with other Samworth businesses, Bradgate is facing broader demands from its customer both in terms of products, but also with an increased emphasis on the use of data and research to understand consumer behaviour and test the validity of propositions. Adapting to these changing needs is an essential part of the ongoing journey in the world of own label supply.

Samworth Brothers' other key sandwich business is Melton Foods, located on the same site in Melton Mowbray as the Group Centre, and built at the same time in the late 1990s. Originally created to produce sandwiches for Waitrose, it still has that business — and indeed has become the principal point of contact for Waitrose across the whole group, but it also produces sandwiches for Ginsters and Costco, and in recent years for Costa Coffee, a key contract win as it represented the first business for Samworth Brothers within the huge coffee chain market.

Managing Director Mary-Ann Kilby has led Melton since 2012. "The Costa win has been huge for us. Due to this development and other business wins we have more than doubled our headcount from 400 up to 900, and we don't have the facilities — changing rooms or a restaurant — to cope with that many, so we are going to invest a significant sum this year to upgrade our facilities."

Mary-Ann Kilby, formerly Sales Director of Saladworks, is also the lead Samworth Brothers executive for Waitrose across the whole Group with collaboration becoming increasingly important. "For example," says Mary-Ann Kilby, "a number of our businesses do party food for Waitrose. The priority now is to show a unified approach from all the Samworth Brothers businesses involved."

Another, different, example of organic growth is the emergence of Brooksby Foods. Initially a satellite to Kettleby, it is now run as a separate business with a strong focus on business innovation. Ian Arnold, former Managing Director of Kettleby Foods, created the embryonic Brooksby Foods, originally called Pate Road, in 2010.

"At Kettleby, our ability to innovate was restricted by our technical standards," says Ian. "For example, we couldn't handle either raw protein or raw leaf. Say we wanted to put a sprig of coriander into something to give extra flavour and pungency — we couldn't do so. So we scoured the country looking for a suitable site to act as an innovation centre — we went to Runcorn, to Milton Keynes — and then, bizarrely, an estate agent's details came across my desk for a unit 800 metres away. It was manna from heaven. It used to be a distribution warehouse for a toyshop in Melton Mowbray — an empty warehouse. We converted the building and created Brooksby Foods in 2010, initially as an offshoot of Kettleby." The new unit marked a different approach to growth. This was not a greenfield site but a clever and gradual adaptation of an existing location to respond to new opportunities.

In its first winter it baked and jellied pork pies for Charnwood — helping them through Christmas. It also started to make ready meals — Tesco Finest fish pie, which moved from being cooked fish to raw fish — so the site became experienced in working with raw protein. The site also helped launch a new stir fry range that included raw spinach and coriander and introduced the site to handling raw leaf.

Eventually it was felt that a developing Brooksby needed more focus. Ian Arnold left Kettleby to take over with a second brief, to also focus on M&A activity, reporting to Lindsey Pownall, for the Group as a whole. "As long as it was seen as an add-on to Kettleby, Brooksby would never get enough focus to make it as profitable as it could be," said Ian Arnold. "So we decided to spin it off, give it its own management team. Lindsey Pownall said: 'Look, you have a reputation for being a bit of a maverick. Let's use that and do things in a different way'."

As well as making ready meals for Tesco, Brooksby has become a place where experiments with new product lines and categories, and routes to market can be tried out. "We see our role as pioneering different routes to market." says Ian Arnold. "We're small enough to be flexible and we're not fixated on one sector." For instance when Lindsey wanted the Group to explore more fried opportunities, we took the fry line out of Tamar. We now do liquid filled fishcakes for Tesco and we're looking at other products."

Those other product opportunities include areas where the Samworth Brothers Group has little or no experience. One of the core objectives of the Brooksby team is to have a balanced amount of its turnover with the major high street retailers. It has launched a range of ready meals for babies and kids with baby food expert Annabelle Karmel, and also a range of Fast Diet Kitchen products alongside 5/2 diet pioneer Dr Michael Mosley and his publishers Short Books. "I think I have the best job in the whole of Samworth Brothers," says Ian Arnold.

Another development in 2015 has been the launch of a new era for Samworth Brothers Distribution. The changes include a new name, Samworth Brothers Supply Chain.

ABOVE: *Brooksby Foods has become a centre for product innovation.*

Although conventional business wisdom says that a company of Samworth Brothers' size should not be operating its own distribution fleet, there can be no doubt that the existence of Samworth Brothers Supply Chain is a vital cog in the chain.

"Outsourcing of logistics is still the dominant model, not only in the food business, but across industry in general," says Samworth Brothers Supply Chain Finance Director David Lynch. "Our differentiator is the same as it always was: we are right at the leading edge of service provision. Other firms that are distributing into the retailers look at us and they recognise that our service levels are significantly higher than anyone else's."

One reason for the name change is that Samworth Brothers Supply Chain better reflects the full range of services that the business is looking to offer the Samworth Brothers Group and its retail partners.

"30 per cent of what we do is external work," says David Lynch. "We mitigate our costs by doing two types of third party work — firstly, we'll consolidate third party loads with Samworth Brothers — that may mean finding other suppliers going into a retailer and consolidating their work so our vehicles are full. And then, when our vehicles get to a depot, they've clearly got to come back, so we'll try to find loads they can carry on the way back. We are also looking to bring raw materials back into the bakeries."

"The other thing that has changed is that we have begun to use subcontractors. Rather than every delivery going on a Samworth Brothers

ABOVE: *In 2015 Samworth Brothers Distribution became Samworth Brothers Supply Chain and launched a new livery.*

vehicle, if we can't get a load to come back, we might use a third party subcontractor. That's a fundamental change in the past 18 months, but it helps to make us more efficient and takes a lorry off the road, with obvious environment benefits."

The distribution industry is currently facing a national driver shortage in the UK. It isn't the most glamorous thing to do, so not so many young people are coming into the business, and therefore the age profile of the Samworth Brothers Supply Chain drivers is increasing. The business is working on a number of initiatives including a new driver academy and a 'warehouse to wheels' programme along with driving training initiatives to alleviate this issue and ensure it has a robust supply of high quality, skilled drivers for the future.

With the launch of the Ginsters Van Sales Company as a separate business, also in 2015, the Group is firmly committed to more innovation in logistics and distribution.

So as the Group moves forward it's clear growth will come from many different sources: acquisition, organic growth in existing businesses and the development of new, adjacent opportunities. When asked to sum up what she believes the future will bring, Group Chief Executive Lindsey Pownall says there is a strong, strategic vision in place. "This is a business with a long and distinguished history but there is a lot more to come. We have always been a growth business and that ambition is still there. The last couple of years have seen a lot of change in the Group and a lot of hard work to get the business in the right place to move forward and start another exciting chapter. I think we are really on our way and there are some exciting times ahead. We've seen some parts of the business experience strong organic growth over the past few years and I am confident this will continue. But we will also be branching out into new directions that fit with our existing competencies.

"We also want to grow without compromise to our values. This book has been commissioned to celebrate Sir David Samworth's 80th birthday. One of the great achievements of Sir David, his brother John and their colleagues in a different era was how they grew the business, without ever losing sight of the values that had guided them through the years and that helped to make the business so special. That has been their great legacy to us and it is our responsibility to cherish it."

A RESPONSIBLE BUSINESS

The most important contribution any business can make to its surrounding communities is to be strong and successful, to provide employment and other opportunities. However a responsible business goes further than this. It wants to play an active and positive role in its local community.

LEFT: *Competitors set off at the 2013 Charity Challenge which took place in Scotland.*

RIGHT: *The Samworth Brothers Sports Opportunity Fund celebrates its first ever award in March 2014 to the Leicester Warriors basketball club. Pictured third and fourth from right are Tim Barker, Samworth Brothers Company Secretary and Sports Opportunity Fund Trustee and Stephen Draisey, Sports Opportunity Fund Chairman.*

Community engagement has been a Samworth Brothers signature for many years. The company has always encouraged its business units to be active parts of their local communities — Ginsters, for example, is a major supporter of charities such as the Royal Voluntary Service, Help for Heroes and CHICKS (Country Holidays for Inner City Kids). The family trust has for some years donated a proportion of its income to charitable causes, including education in Africa, and campaigning to stop human trafficking and assist those who have been trafficked.

There is always a strong sense in the Group that, as Mark Samworth says, the biggest contribution any business can make to its surrounding communities is to be successful. "The biggest impact we can have on communities is running strong businesses. So our first focus has to be getting the strong commercial message right. What's best about this business is that it provides employment and livelihood to a lot of people," he says.

BELOW: *Cotehele Gig Club members and supporters congregate as the club's new gig 'Teylu' is launched into the River Tamar from Cotehele Quay. The gig was funded by a grant from The Samworth Brothers Sports Opportunity Fund so the Club can offer more rowing opportunities for young people. Teylu is the Cornish word for family.*

BELOW (LEFT): *Ginsters staff on a day out helping the CHICKS childrens' holiday charity spruce up its facilities.*

However in recent years the Group's charitable and community activities have developed and now divide into three main areas, site specific activity at each of the businesses, plus two main corporate activities, the Samworth Brothers Sports Opportunity Fund and the Samworth Brothers Charity Challenge.

Across the Group all the businesses have strong relationships with local community groups and charities. The range of activity is extremely varied but includes many valuable partnerships that are making a real difference in the community. In Leicestershire many of the businesses have a close link with the charity Leicestershire Cares. Samworth Brothers' staff donate time to help literacy and numeracy projects for primary and secondary school children, and support other Leicestershire Cares projects such as hosting bakery tours for the Flying Fish project that helps young care leavers find their way in the world. The company is also a Patron of The Prince's Trust and staff volunteers help disadvantaged youngsters with CV writing and interviewing technique through a Trust scheme. In Cornwall, Ginsters and Tamar have worked with a youth offending scheme to deliver employability training. Ginsters also supports Plymouth-based charity Shekinah Mission.

In terms of Group initiatives former Executive Board Director Stephen Draisey oversees the Sports Opportunity Fund. "We used to

ABOVE: *Dean Spencer (centre left), Samworth Brothers staff member and volunteer at a Leicester based boxing club Gunn's Gym, celebrates a Samworth Brothers Sports Opportunity award for his club. The club was given £1,000 to help extend the motivational bronze, silver and gold award scheme that Dean devised and has helped to run for the past 10 years.*

ABOVE: *Tim Barker, Samworth Brothers Sports Opportunity Trustee and Group Company Secretary at an award presentation to the Mount Group for the Disabled charity based in Somerby, near Melton Mowbray. A Sports Opportunity award allowed the club to buy Jet, (also pictured), a mechanical horse that helps the young club members improve their riding skills.*

give a proportion of our profits to our family charitable foundation," says Mark Samworth. "We wanted to give our people more say in how this money was spent. So we created the Sports Opportunity Fund, which is all about local communities and putting something back."

The Fund made its first grant in 2013. "Mark approached me, via Lindsey, 18 months ago, to say that he now wanted the business to look after this programme," says Stephen Draisey. "The sums are considerable — about half a million pounds a year. He wanted the money channelled to local organisations that would help young people get on through sport — either physically, or via increased self esteem. I said, that's the hardest job I have ever been given!

"We formed a small group — me, Tim Barker, Joanne Milroy, our Communication Director, and we recruited Lisa Wainwright, who is head of Volleyball England. What we have done is set up two types of awards. We give up to £1,000 for causes nominated by staff members — for example we have two staff members, a husband and wife, who help run a local boxing club. We gave them money to fund a prize evening and some kit. And then there are larger grants — we gave £25,000 to the Leicester Warriors basketball club, which is totally run

by volunteers, to help them with hardship money for kids who couldn't afford to come and play, and to develop their coaching skills. The Waterfront Boxing Club in Leicester needed some money to help do up their premises and help train volunteers. We've done a scheme with a commander of Leicestershire Police — along with Leicester City FC. The police came to us and said, 'we've profiled 40 youngsters. If we don't intervene, we will soon be arresting them for drug dealing, arson and the like. With the football club, we want to set up a scheme to get them off the streets and divert them away from crime.' And we've spent £12,000 on a horse simulator for a riding school for disabled children in Melton Mowbray." A number of Cornish awards have also been made including the funding of a new Cornish gig, or rowing boat, for

ABOVE: *The Samworth Brothers Charity Challenge has raised more than £1.1 million for charity to date with the 2015 Challenge, taking place as this book went to press, expected to boost the total even further.*

ABOVE: *Competitors line up for the rowing leg of the 2013 Charity Challenge in glorious weather on Loch Lomond.*

the Cotehele Gig Club, near Callington, to provide more access for young people to the popular Cornish sport of gig rowing and support for the Launceston Junior Hockey Team and Plymouth YMCA.

The second big Samworth Brothers community activity is the Charity Challenge, which was created by Lindsey Pownall when she was in charge of Bradgate Bakery, and which has already raised over a million pounds. "I am hugely proud of the Charity Challenge," she says. "A few years ago, I took my team from Bradgate to do some teambuilding in the Lake District. It was great, and I met some people in the world of the outdoors. One of them said to me, have you ever thought of doing something along these lines to raise money for charity. I thought that was a great idea and I decided to do something with Bradgate Bakery, Saladworks and Melton Foods — the businesses I chaired. Brian Stein said he had no objection, so I said 'Shall I offer it to the whole Group?'

He said yes. I designed the event and personally ran it. It was a huge success." After two events in the Lake District, the third Challenge in 2011 was held in Cornwall and was run by Mark Duddridge, the fourth in 2013 in Scotland, with Paul Davey leading the organisation. And in 2015, Anil Ahir took responsibility for the Challenge, in mid-Wales. Paul Davey is now the Group Executive Board member responsible for the fund raising platform, the Charity Challenge.

Any responsible business is also increasingly concerned about its environmental footprint. Over the years many Samworth Brothers businesses have had strong environmental and energy saving programmes in place. However in the last few years, the company has realised it needs to coordinate these activities from the centre.

Deborah Carlin joined as Group Sustainability Advisor in 2013. "The Group Technical Director, Mark Shippey, identified that our

ABOVE: *Samworth Brothers Group Chief Executive Lindsey Pownall (right) and Charity Challenge organiser Paul Davey (left) with Olympic and World Triathlon champions Alistair and Jonny Brownlee presenting a cheque for £30,000 to the Loch Lomond Mountain Rescue Team.*

TOP: *Competitors set off on the mountain leg of the 2013 Charity Challenge.*

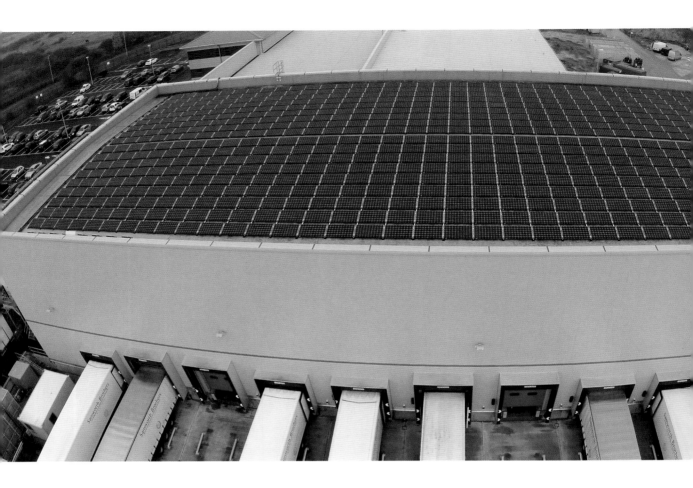

major retail customers were asking more and more questions about sustainability and that Tesco, in particular, had started a journey in terms of carbon management — so Samworth Brothers needed someone at Group level," says Deborah Carlin. "Most of the businesses were doing something around energy, but not necessarily in a structured manner. What we're trying to do now is provide a steer in terms of our Group priorities. What we're looking at right now is environmental management — energy, water, waste and an environmental management system to capture all our impacts. The other side is ethical — responsible sourcing and how we manage our people. It will branch out into the community element also."

"Ginsters is ahead of the game," she goes on. "They have their own environmental manager on site — being sustainable is a part of their brand values. They were the first in their industry to use palm oil

ABOVE: *Solar panels at Ashton Green.*

ABOVE (RIGHT): *22% of the Ashton Green site's energy is generated from renewable resources, such as waste heat energy from the bakery's refrigeration units.*

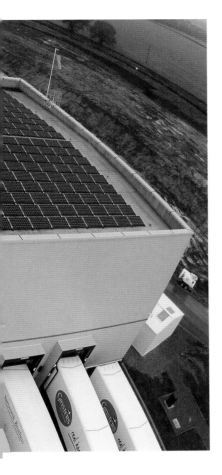

approved by the Roundtable on Sustainable Palm Oil, which focuses on ensuring that farmers are not cutting down rainforest to plant palm oil. Now, retailers are starting to ask for that, and our other sites are working towards the same goal. "When I first started, the question I was asked at every business was 'Tell me what sustainability is?' As soon as you start talking about managing environmental impacts, energy, waste, water, people, communities, they would say 'Yes, we're doing that'. We're particularly strong on the community element, while environmentally, there's always more to do, and things are happening in pockets rather than Group wide."

The recent build of the new Ashton Green site has given the Group a chance to make a real statement on sustainability. The facility has been designed from the ground up with environmental management in mind, with 22% of the site's energy being generated from renewable resources, including a 200kW solar array system on the roof of the building. In addition an energy efficient water source heat pump that captures waste heat energy from the bakery's refrigeration units is also contributing to the renewable energy total.

THIS PAGE: *Sir David Samworth visiting one of the three Samworth Academy schools.*

OPPOSITE: *Samworth Brothers Annual General Meeting, June 2014 at Bradgate Bakery.*

VALUES

Any business is a living, breathing entity that changes over time. The current
Group is very different from even its counterpart of five years ago, let alone
10, 20 or 30 years gone by. However there is always one constant through the
years, the strong values that the business has been built on.

David Samworth was knighted in the 2009 Birthday Honours List, in recognition of his extensive charitable work, including the creation of three Academy schools in Leicestershire and Nottinghamshire but, he says, he views the award in a much broader context. "I would never have been in a position to receive that award if it weren't for all the people I have worked with throughout my life," he says. "So I see the knighthood as being a recognition for the business as a whole."

It may be ten years since he retired from active participation in the life of Samworth Brothers, but the values Sir David laid down remain at the heart of how the Group still operates and, as many people in the various different businesses will testify, his influence is still strong. "Sir David has taken a back seat, but in the last two or three years, Mark has really stepped into that role," says Ian Arnold of Brooksby Foods.

BELOW: *President Moi of Kenya and David Samworth, visiting as President of the Royal Agricultural Society of England in 2001. Watching is National President Mrs Ann Womba.*

"And Sir David is still intimately involved with the business. I went
over to Chetwode last week, bumped into Sir David, and he asked me
how my numbers were. He knew how my numbers were! He wanted
to see how I answered the question. You still feel that the family's passion for the business is still there. At the AGM, all the family, no matter
where they are in the world, come back, and are totally engaged. You
still dread the phone call on a Friday afternoon saying 'It's Sir David',
because he still panels the products on a weekly basis. He'll panel them,
and he doesn't tend to phone you to tell you how fantastic something
is — but if he's not happy with the bake penetration, he lets you know
straight away!"

Alex Knight, who helped lay down the foundations of the Samworth
Brothers culture back in the 1990s, happily recounts the story of how
he first met Sir David. "We got this phone call one day and my assistant

came in and said 'Alex, I just took a call from a Mr David Samworth who said he has done a review of a number of different consultancies and has decided to choose you and are you free next Tuesday to go and meet them'," he says. "Being David, they'd done an absolutely thorough job, without telling anyone! At that time David was CEO, he was Chairman, he was Managing Director and probably Production Director of several things too."

Holdings Board Director William Kendall, who joined the board recently, says the commitment of the Group to its culture is clear to see. "I was asked if I was interested in talking to Samworth Brothers, and I had a preliminary chat with Nick Linney and Mark Samworth," he says. "From an hour's chat, I picked up very clearly what the Group

ABOVE: *In 2009 David Samworth was knighted for services to charity. Pictured, Sir David at a visit to the Samworth Academy in Nottingham in 2010.*

ABOVE (LEFT): *Sir David in the uniform of a Deputy Lieutenant of Leicestershire.*

is about — the commitment to quality is obvious. But also, they understand the importance of people. To be successful as you grow, you have to create a culture where every employee feels as though they are running their own business. Family businesses are a good opportunity to do that — people live in families, so working in families makes sense. If the owners treat their employees like part of their extended family it is hardly surprising that the people are committed and put in that bit extra. But with Samworth Brothers, there's something more. I remember my first Group AGM. I came into the room and David was there. He said, 'William, I want you to meet someone', and he introduced me to a guy from Ginsters who'd been there since before they bought the place and who did the garden. That said a lot to me."

Chairman Nick Linney believes that government and others are now recognising the value of the family business. "Family businesses are louder and prouder than they were ten years ago," he says. "For the first time in my working life, a British government has come to the conclusion that it is medium sized businesses that create jobs and drive economic growth. The family business sector is being seen as an economic engine."

Nick Linney also recognises it has been a period of change for Samworth Brothers. "We have been through the corporate equivalent of the Sixties. Suddenly someone threw the jigsaw up in the air and the pieces came down looking all different. Now, the operational style of the business is radically different."

"The only thing that is inviolate is our culture," continues Nick Linney. "For us to be able to change the business, the people in it have to believe that we are fair-minded, canny, clever people. If we fail on those counts, the changes we put in place will fail."

As this book illustrates, previous Samworth generations adapted well to shifts in the business landscape, whether that be wartime, high inflation periods, the rise of the multiple retail chains or other events. In just the same way the Group is responding to the challenges of today. Consumers are shopping in new ways that in 2014 and 2015 has had a significant impact on the UK retail market. After years of big expansion, a good number of the Group's retail customers are now operating in a lower growth trading environment. For the Group this

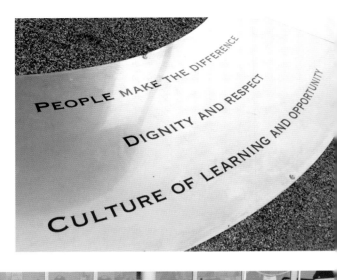

ABOVE: *A Bradgate Foods Long Service Awards event at Leicester racecourse.*

TOP LEFT AND RIGHT: *An external sculpture at the Bradgate Bakery Ashton Green site celebrates the shared values of Samworth Brothers and its customer, Tesco.*

is a new and different set of circumstances that has to be met head on. Customers are wanting more cross company collaboration. They need to see efficiencies and a simplified approach. A big priority for the Group is finding ways to help its retail customers adapt to this 'new normal'. Better collaboration across the Group is one important aspect.

However if the Group is going to continue to grow it will also have to seek out new growth areas and markets to invest in, either through organic growth or acquisitions. "Change is here to stay," says Lindsey

Pownall. "What will enable us to succeed in the future is getting good at change and realising that nothing is beyond us. David started this business, but when you start something you don't know where it is going to go. And our journey is not finished, not by a long way. David's gift to us is our values. Inevitably the actual operations have morphed away from the business that he ran, but we still live and die by the values that he laid down. As long as I am here, that is the one thing that will not change."

ABOVE: *Quality has always been at the heart of Samworth Brothers. A team from Walker & Son celebrate a prestigious Q (for quality) Award for their Marks & Spencer Whole Baked Pear and Stilton Pork Pie.*

Appendices

Appendix 1

Introduction to the 2005 edition of *A Way of Life*

By David Samworth CBE, DL

Appendix 2

'Into the next millennium' by David Samworth CBE, DL, which formed the final chapter of the first edition of this book, published as *A Taste of Tradition* in 1996.

Appendix 3

Foreword to the First Edition of this book by The Rt Hon The Lord Walker of Worcester MBE PC, published as *A Taste of Tradition* in 1996.

Appendix 1

Introduction to the 2005 edition of A Way of Life
By David Samworth CBE, DL

When my grandfather started his own business in 1896, he could no more imagine how it would look today than I can conceive of how Samworth Brothers might look in another hundred years' time. So whatever the future holds, I am immensely proud to have spent my life in a business that I believe can last through the generations.

This year sees my retirement from Samworth Brothers — an event some thought might never happen! The people I leave behind are the best in the industry, and they have helped build a business that is innovative, well invested and that continues to seek quality in everything it does. When I look around our Group and see 12 businesses producing high quality foods for the most discerning (and sometimes the most aggressive) markets in the world, I see our people doing it with a passion that I have always felt was one of the hallmarks of Samworth Brothers.

I am proud that we have been able to maintain our ethos of quality across the Group. We demonstrate the same passion for our products at Ginsters, a £200 million nationally distributed brand, as we do when we hand-raise our pies at Dickinson & Morris, the oldest remaining producer of Melton Mowbray pork pies in that famous town. I am convinced that the business has every chance of long-term success if it maintains this attitude. It has always been our belief that consumers will not accept a lower quality of food as time goes by, indeed that the opposite is in fact true. As consumers, we all want better and better standards of service and quality, and those businesses that can continually improve their products will be the ones that thrive. I can think of no successful brand or business that has prospered in the long term by lowering its standards.

The culture that is the heart of Samworth Brothers is rooted in the values of our family. My brothers Frank, John and I were raised in a household where working in a family business was seen as a part of our heritage, even after the Government had put an end to our pig dealing business in 1939 and before my father bought TN Parr in 1950. The values and attitudes that have stayed with us throughout our lives were instilled in us around the kitchen table — what we learned about the value of money, the importance of quality and the need to see people do well in their lives has been translated into the 'People, Quality, Profit' approach of the business today. For my part, I have always tried to pass on the same values to my children.

In the first edition of this book, I wrote a chapter entitled 'Into the Next Millennium' which described my thoughts about Samworth Brothers at the time and made some mention of how our culture created a unified business. Reading it again today, I am pleased to say that it is as true now as when it was written in 1996. The original chapter has been included as an Appendix to this edition, and I hope that you will read it.

John and I could not foresee the scale of the business as it is today — my father bought a business with 15 people in 1950, and we now employ more than 5,500. We modelled Ginsters (and later Walkers) around the idea of producing the very best products we could and then seeing how far the business could go. When we bought Ginsters in 1978, its turnover was £1 million. The first edition of this book reported the group's 1995 sales as £116 million, and it spoke with feeling about our 2,300 staff. With this second edition, published not ten years later, our sales stand at more than £450 million and we have created an additional 3,200 jobs. The last ten years have seen extraordinary growth, have put Samworth Brothers in the spotlight as a leader in the industry and have seen it recognised as Leicestershire's Business of the Decade.

Yet it did not have to be like this. Success was never guaranteed at any time in our firm's history, and any future success is no more certain now than it was when I joined the business in 1956. Samworth Brothers will continue to face significant and often daunting challenges from competitors, customers and the external world, but I hope that our culture will help us see the opportunities and make the right decisions for profitable growth in the future. When I look back on my career, I remember the dual purchase of William Watson's and Pork Farms in 1969, which strained our finances to breaking point; the government price control and profit margin restrictions in the early 1970s;

the oil crisis and three day week of 1973/74 and many other such challenges, and I feel reassured that there is no limit to what good people and a strong culture can achieve, whatever the external environment throws at a business.

The purpose of this book is to act both as a record of the history of my family's business and as a learning tool for those who may be interested in it. It is certainly not the case that what we can justifiably describe as a successful business today is merely the inevitable result of either our dedication to our culture, or the growth of the supermarkets, or even of the decisions taken by people at key stages in our history, although all have played their part. Rather, it is about people applying common sense to situations, being guided not by the dogmatic application of inflexible principles but by an understanding of what they could achieve, and it is about those people working hard to get results. Ultimately, Samworth Brothers owes its position in the market today to a large number of individuals who saw opportunities in the market and took them. Many such people are named in the book but I particularly want to mention my father Frank Senior, my brothers John and Frank, the latter of whom sadly died while this new edition was in production, the late Ken Parr, the Ginster family, the late Gerry Gerrard, the boards of Ginsters and Walkers (led by Denis Kearney and Bryan Skelston) who established a platform for our growth, and Brian Stein and his team today. Our Group today produces not only the pies, hams, sausages and pasties which made up the core of our sales in the early 1990s, but also desserts, sandwiches (we are the world's second largest producer), British and Italian ready meals, savoury slices, salads and other great food products which have provided growth for the business and opportunities for the people in it. Organic growth such as we have seen in Samworth Brothers depends on the vision and drive of individuals, and maintaining our entrepreneurial spirit will be a key challenge for the future.

It will be a test of the business in the years to come, then, to see how it manages its scale without losing the ability to motivate and satisfy the needs of its people. I hope that our decentralised structure will continue to provide each business with the benefits of belonging to a larger federation while allowing them the freedom to think locally, act quickly and be creative in their outlook. Many of our competitors are doing the reverse, driven by the short-term demands of the stock market. They are centralising, creating unwieldy divisional structures and taking authority away from the people at the sharp end of their business. For me, this demonstrates not only an erosion of responsibility, authority and opportunity away from the key people in the business, but also an erosion of trust that will take many years to overcome. I believe that remaining private is a key competitive advantage for Samworth Brothers, and the ability to structure our business to avoid such damaging centralisation is a good example of the real difference that being a family business can make. Ultimately, a company is only as good as its people, and I hope that Samworth Brothers can continue to develop and reward its people and that they, in turn, will continue to drive the company forward.

Appendix 2

'Into the next millennium' by David Samworth CBE, DL, which formed the final chapter of the first edition of this book, published as A Taste of Tradition *in 1996.*

The history of our family and our business has only one benchmark with which to judge us: Quality. In the course of the last century, change has been as dramatic as it has been inevitable. In the 1890s we were driving pigs through the centre of Birmingham on their way to butchers' shops, and in the 1990s we are building highly automated bakeries, using the latest in computer-aided design, to make fresh products en route to some of the most discerning and sophisticated supermarkets in the world.

During my business career, our sales and profits have been earned at one time or another from retailing, from bacon curing, from van selling, from producing retailers' own brands and added to the list now is the marketing of our own manufactured brands. Each of these stages entailed a major change in direction for the company. But, in spite of these very different activities over the years, it is not the changes that impress me so much as that which has endured and been strengthened; the emphasis on People, Quality and Profit.

The appreciation of quality is always the first thing we look for in any person who joins our organisation. There are many who will measure quality against a specification, or against whatever the customer has asked for, but it is the few who have a genuine feel for the product and a real passion for its continuous improvement that we welcome as colleagues.

The company owes its early success to such people as my grandfather, George Samworth, my father, Frank Samworth Senior, my brothers Frank and John, Gerry Gerrard, Ken Parr, the Ginster family and many more. People have given the company the quality culture that sets it apart from the many others and it is people that are the business's most important asset. It is true that a business can be more than the sum of its assets, but without quality-minded people our company would cease to exist.

It is because the feel for quality exists within people and not within testing laboratories or measurement charts that people at all levels play the defining role in the company. Our standards are high, and occasionally we do not live up to our wish to put the selection, training and care of our people at the centre of our business. So we are working harder than ever to do so and to ensure that everyone in our group is treated with dignity and respect at all times. It is a journey without end, down a road we have committed ourselves to follow with the utmost determination.

We share a love of our products and never cease in our quest to try and find ways to improve their eating qualities. But it is not just the quality of our products which we seek to improve. Our buildings, their surrounding grounds, staff restaurants, changing facilities, vehicles, plant and machinery must all be better with every new year. Quality is indeed a way of life, and must be pursued in every aspect of it.

Care and commitment to our people combined with a passion for improving quality is not sufficient to cope with our growth in the future; we need profits and the cashflow associated with them. We have developed a circle of good people producing good products which earn profits and generate the cashflow, the vast majority of which in turn is reinvested in new products and facilities. Profits are essential if we, as a group of companies, are to meet the changing demands in a rapidly changing world, and essential if future generations of consumers are to have the quality products they deserve.

People, Quality and Profit are the principles that create the ethos by which our business thrives. They have not changed over the last century and will not change as we progress towards the new millennium, and I am convinced of Samworth Brothers Limited's future success so long as it keeps, throughout the federation of its companies, this philosophy at the centre of all its activities.

As our business grows, so our responsibility to our employees and the communities in which we operate becomes ever greater. We will, at all times, behave ethically and show loyalty to our 2,300 colleagues, and it is these considerations above all else that has encouraged John and me to develop a business that is as stable as it is strong. The majority of family businesses never outlive the founding generation. Ours, with Mark, is entering the fourth generation and this is testament to the foresight of those who have gone before us. Over recent years we have been building one of the best and most professional systems of governance that I have seen in a private business.

As we approach the next millennium, and on the 100th anniversary of our business, I am pleased that we are as professional in our dealings as a public company and as single-minded in vision, and as quickly adaptable in its execution as the smallest of family firms. Keeping this balance will give us competitive advantage and ensure that the quality that the company yearns for is not lost in management succession or short-term demands from shareholders.

There are many measurements of the strength of a business; money in the bank, strong profitability and a good cashflow, along with an envied reputation as employers, manufacturers and suppliers, may all point to a company in good health with exciting prospects. Yet my final measure of our family company is the pride I feel when talking to any one of 2,300 of my colleagues.

I am proud when I hear of the awards their hard work has won them, I am proud when they tell me of the success of their companies, and I am proud when they tell me that they produce the finest quality in the market. But more than any of these, I take pride in enjoying the food we produce. Our company, like our family, gives me pride and so I know both are strong.

Appendix 3

Foreword to the First Edition of this book by The Rt Hon The Lord Walker of Worcester MBE PC, published as A Taste of Tradition *in 1996.*

I am delighted that A Taste of Tradition has been written. It is an enjoyable read but, perhaps even more important, it is a fabulous story of the achievements of one family over the last century.

George Samworth, when he was working 65 hours a week for ten shillings (50p) a week selling pigs to the pork butchers of Birmingham, would have been very surprised if he had been told that a hundred years later his family, having sold one business for £23 millon, would be leading and controlling another business with a turnover of £150 million.

The importance of this book is that it is a marvellous illustration of a family business, providing of course it is a family that keeps up to date, adjusts to the times and has a constant desire to keep a high quality control.

When I first had the privilege of visiting one of the factories producing the traditional pork pie, one was impressed firstly by the total cleanliness, secondly the constant control of the production line and thirdly the cheerfulness of all those that were employed there. You left knowing that here was a well-managed business.

As a former Minister of Agriculture, I was well aware of the transformation that was taking place in the food industries throughout the world. The move of business from the small grocers shop to the supermarket, the ever-increasing demand for convenience food and the strict control to see that the high standards of hygiene were achieved.

These radical changes meant the disappearance of many smaller businesses. To the Samworth family, it was a challenge to be met with enthusiasm, a challenge that offered new opportunities and not a reason to decline.

As David, John and Mark continue to lead the business, one knows it will be a continuing story of growth, innovation and the best possible quality control.

As somebody who had the privilege of being a member of most British Cabinets in the 1970s and 1980s, my only regret is that there are not many more families like the Samworths. My pleasure at the publication of this book is that I hope that many of our younger generation will learn from the accumulated wisdom of this family and apply that wisdom to the future.

Index